DATE			

Mark Twain

LIVES AND LEGACIES

Larzer Ziff
MARK TWAIN

David S. Reynolds
WALT WHITMAN

Craig T. Raine
T. S. ELIOT

MARK TWAIN

Larzer Ziff

OXFORD
UNIVERSITY PRESS

2004

OXFORD
UNIVERSITY PRESS

Oxford   New York
Auckland   Bangkok   Buenos Aires   Cape Town   Chennai
Dar es Salaam   Delhi   Hong Kong   Istanbul   Karachi   Kolkata
Kuala Lumpur   Madrid   Melbourne   Mexico City   Mumbai   Nairobi
São Paulo   Shanghai   Taipei   Tokyo   Toronto

Copyright © 2004 by Larzer Ziff

Published by Oxford University Press, Inc.
198 Madison Avenue, New York, New York 10016
www.oup.com

Oxford is a registered trademark of Oxford University Press

Library of Congress Cataloging-in-Publication Data

Ziff, Larzer, 1927–
Mark Twain / Larzer Ziff.
p. cm.
Includes bibliographical references and index.
ISBN 0-19-517019-9
1. Twain, Mark, 1835–1910.
2. Authors, American—19th century—Biography.
I. Title.
PS1331.Z54 2004
818'.409—dc22   2004003034

3 5 7 9 8 6 4 2

Printed in the United States of America
on acid-free paper

Contents

Samuel L. Clemens, Esq., Doctor of Letters (Oxford, 1907).
Courtesy, The Mark Twain Project, The Bancroft Library

MARK TWAIN

One

CELEBRITY

Sᴀᴍ Cʟᴇᴍᴇɴꜱ ʙᴇɢᴀɴ ᴛʜᴇ ᴅᴇᴄᴀᴅᴇ ᴏꜰ ᴛʜᴇ 1850ꜱ ᴀꜱ ᴀ ʜᴇʟᴘᴇʀ ɪɴ ᴛʜᴇ office of his brother Orion's newspaper, the *Western Union*. He was fifteen and had been out of school since he was eleven. He ended the decade as an unemployed steamboat pilot, the Civil War having closed down commerce between North and South on the great highway of the Mississippi River.

During that same decade American literary culture came of age with the appearance of works by Nathaniel Hawthorne, Herman Melville, Henry David Thoreau, Harriet Beecher Stowe, and Walt Whitman that have since been regarded as classics of the national literature. The prophet of that renaissance, Ralph Waldo Emerson, continued throughout the 1850s to serve as its intellectual leader, carrying his message to lecture halls as well as publishing it in essays. "Our days of dependence, our long apprenticeship to the learning of other lands, draws to a close," he had announced in 1837. "The millions that around us are rushing into life, cannot always be fed on the sere remains of foreign harvests." The literary consequences of this declaration of the independence of American culture mark the time as the Age of Emerson. That age ended with the Civil War, and the seismic shift in American life that followed in the second half of the century brought on the Age of Mark Twain.

Emerson and his contemporaries were citizens of a country that was still essentially agricultural, and the emerging industrialism of the nation was to be glimpsed only in the margins of their writings, if at all. One senses an authorial fascination, part wonder and part worry, as the railroad passes Walden Pond or winds away from the house of the seven gables into the countryside; and although Melville does describe the dehumanized working conditions of women factory hands, he turns the description into an allegory of their physiological rather than their economic entrapment. The free states that Stowe contrasts with slave states in *Uncle Tom's Cabin* are presented as agricultural even though advocates of the southern cause were then asserting that the North was attacking chattel slavery on the plantation only to protect wage slavery in the factory.

As the great literary decades of the 1850s closed, industrial output in the United States lagged behind that of Great Britain, France, and Germany, while the agricultural American South was a region of such wealth that had the impending move toward secession succeeded, economic historians estimate, the independent Confederacy would have been the fourth richest country in the world. Yet only forty years later the industrial production of the United States surpassed the *combined* manufactures of its three main rivals.[1]

Born into the agricultural, slaveholding South in 1835, Mark Twain rose to prominence in the second half of the nineteenth century, his achievement and his fame growing in step with the fast-flying industrial development that enthralled him with its inventiveness, technical efficiency, and quickening accumulation of riches. A critical observer of the nation's transformation from farm to factory, Twain was also an eager participant in the process, lured time and again into investing in one or another project that held forth the prospect of enormous wealth. The large-scale production that accompanied industrialization also affected the publishing industry, and his writings benefited from new techniques for the marketing of books to the large population of readers who were not as yet book owners, while he himself became a publisher as well as a writer of books for the many.

But comfortable as was the fortune he gained from his great artistry and his mastery of the publishing profession, Twain was an obsessive investor in one or another contrivance that promised to produce profits on a scale of millions of dollars rather than the tens of thousands his own work earned him. One after another invention—such as a new kind of steam generator, or steam pulley, or marine telegraph, or engraving process—drew never-to-be-seen-again dollars from his pocket, while, with what seemed a genius for miscalculation, he turned down an opportunity to back Alexander Graham Bell's contrivance for speaking over a distance. As a veteran journeyman printer himself, he understood the fortune to be made by developing a machine that would set and redistribute type automatically. Then all too characteristically, Twain backed the fragile and inordinately complex Paige machine, in his confidence declining to hedge his bet by exchanging some of his stock for an interest in the Merganthaler linotype machine that was to drive the Paige machine off the market and him into bankruptcy. Intoxicated with what he called "the drive and push and rush and struggle of the living, tearing, booming nineteenth, the mightiest of all the centuries!"[2] it was, he said, "the only century worth living in since time itself was invented."[3] He recklessly participated in its excesses even as he exposed them to ridicule in his writings.

In the first half of the century, writers such as Emerson and Hawthorne remained personally apart from what their writings criticized as socially disgraceful, if not downright immoral, and their prose, correspondingly, was literary—different in tone and diction from the speech of those engaged in what Thoreau characterized as lives of quiet desperation. In the latter half of the century Twain, who entered enthusiastically into the values of a culture marked by aggressive commercial practice and hungering social aspiration, wrote, correspondingly, in the vernacular of those immersed in the hurly-burly; that is, in the speech of Americans. His success in making that speech achieve subtle moral effects through humor revolutionized American literary expression, and in the wake of his achievement colloquial language shed the quotation marks it had previously worn to quarantine it from contaminating the literary language of the text and became the tongue of the American writer.

Alert Yankee that he was, Emerson had an inkling of what was about to happen. He was in the upper Midwest in the cold January of 1856 bringing his transcendental message to the farmers, loggers, and hunters of the region. One evening when one of his audience walked out of the hall during a lecture, he returned to his lodging to tell his notebook that, after all, the people are always right and "the man of letters is to say, these are the new conditions to which I must conform. The architect who is asked to build a ship to go upon the sea must not build a parthenon or a square house, but a ship. And Shakespeare or Franklin or Aesop coming to Illinois, would say, I must give my wisdom a comic form, instead of tragics or elegiacs."[4] In that same month twenty-one-year-old Sam Clemens was working as a journeyman printer in Keokuk, Iowa.

John Marshall Clemens, Sam's father, died in Hannibal, Missouri, when Sam (born November 20, 1835) was eleven years old. After some persistent nagging, he gained his mother's permission to leave off attending school in favor of taking a job but also then assuaged her Presbyterian fervor by promising to refrain from imbibing hard spirits, an assurance easily kept at that age and as easily disregarded at a later one. Yet although the promise was broken and in later years he was a vehement critic of Christian, especially missionary, hypocrisy, nevertheless the iron logic of Presbyterian doctrine remained with him throughout his career. In a largely unconscious parallel to the Puritan doctrine of humiliation as the necessary starting step in the salvation experience—first humiliation and then vocation because one must be purged of self-esteem before the call to redemption can come—in his stories the humiliation of the greenhorn (most often his fictionalized self) is always the starting point for the acquisition of mature knowledge. The cub pilot's lessons in "Old Times on the Mississippi" (1875), for example, begin with the master pilot mercilessly holding his ignorance up to ridicule, and the clueless easterner in *Roughing It* (1872) does not participate in the code of the West—become one of the boys—until a series of abashing errors flattens his self-esteem.

Freed from schooling, young Sam Clemens took a variety of odd jobs but soon focused on learning the craft of the printer. As

Melville's Ishmael had said of a whaling ship so with even greater validity Clemens could have said of the print shop: it was his Harvard College and his Yale. By the time he was eighteen he had worked himself up from being an apprentice on Hannibal and other small-town newspapers to serving as a journeyman printer on jobs in St. Louis, New York, and Philadelphia. Most papers, after printing what local news and advertisements there were, filled the remaining space with items copied from other newspapers and magazines, and even then usually had space for any additional material that came to hand from poetizing contributors or from editor and printer wracking their brains for copy to fill up an issue. In this way Sam Clemens began producing stories, sketches, and travel pieces. They were written principally for whatever newspaper in Missouri and later Iowa his dreamy and consistently unsuccessful older brother, Orion, then owned, but he also made submissions to magazines, employing pen names but not yet signing himself "Mark Twain." Even after that name became famous, his transition from printer to writer was never total. Durable memories of the provincial print shops of his youth made a mark on his business career, leading him to become a publisher as well as an author, and, with a keen recollection of the tedious hours he had spent setting and re-distributing type, enticing him to make the heavy investments in the Paige mechanical typesetter that led to his financial ruin.

Print shops and newspapers also kept popping up in his novels: for example, a brief print shop scene in *Huckleberry Finn* (1884), a lengthy—indeed too lengthy—lampoon of frontier newspapers replete with misprints, inverted letters, and broken types in *A Connecticut Yankee in King Arthur's Court* (1889), and even a rather curious, detailed introduction of a print shop into medieval Austria in *The Mysterious Stranger*.[5]

The best of Mark Twain's fanciful improvisations on the printer-journalists of his youth, however, are to be found in his lesser known sketches. "Our usually quiet city of Rome was thrown into a state of wild excitement yesterday by the experience of one of those bloody affrays which sicken the heart and fill the soul with fear, while they inspire all thinking men with forebodings for the future of a city where human life is held so cheaply, and the gravest laws are held in defiance." So begins the conscientious journalistic account of the assassination of Julius Caesar in the "Roman Daily Evening Fasces," a satire on the transparently hypocritical civic piety of western newspapers that reported with relish yet another local murder while professedly regretting it. In sly parallel with its high-minded deploring but actual savoring of the happenings on the street, the portentous prose of long-winded complex sentences and passive verbs is prone to unexpectedly sagging into colloquialism: "We are further informed that there are many among us who think that they are justified in believing that the assassination of Julius Caesar was a put-up thing."[6] That their language betrays the true character of those who are pretending to mean differently was to become a hallmark of Twain's social criticism as well as his fiction.

In 1857 Sam Clemens left print shops behind him for a career as a pilot on the Mississippi River, and so began three years in the profession he ever after maintained was the one he liked above any other he pursued in his lifetime. But, as he wrote, "by and by the war came, commerce was suspended, my occupation was gone. . . . So I became a silver miner in Nevada; next a newspaper reporter; next a gold miner, in California; next a reporter in San

Francisco; next a special correspondent in the Sandwich Islands; next a roving correspondent in Europe and the East; next, an instructional torch-bearer on the lecture platform, and, finally, I became a scribbler of books and an immovable fixture among the rocks of New England."[7]

Each of the phases of the career Twain thus summarized proved a rich field for his fertile imagination. We see Twain as a riverboat pilot in *Life on the Mississippi* (1883), a miner in *Roughing It* (1872), and a newspaper correspondent in *The Innocents Abroad* (1869), to name but three of the nonfiction works based upon his life. Yet in each his creative exuberance roars on past the historical details. As the companion of his last years and authorized biographer, Albert Bigelow Paine said: "Incidents were filtered through his vivid imagination until many of them bore little relation to the actual occurrence."[8] If they cannot be relied upon for accurate biographical information about Samuel Langhorne Clemens, however, these books do tell us everything about Clemens's favorite character, Mark Twain, although it would be wrong to see Mark Twain as only a character in books that bore his name.

Clemens first used the name in 1863 when he was reporting on the doings of the Nevada legislature for the *Virginia City Enterprise*. His articles were popular throughout the region, and many readers knew who wrote them even though their author was not identified in print. But aware of his local popularity and eager to be known to a wider audience, Clemens told his editor that he would like to sign his articles; he chose the name "Mark Twain" because, he said, that river term, the leadman's cry of two fathoms (twelve feet), "has a richness about it; it was always a pleasant sound for a pilot to hear on a dark night; it meant safe water."[9]

Pen names were common in that day, especially among western comic writers, and most often denoted a created personality totally different in character from the person of their creators. For example, the lettered Ohio newspaperman, Charles Farrar Browne, a humorist and comic lecturer whom Clemens knew and greatly admired, wrote his comic pieces as from the pen of "Artemus Ward," an itinerant impresario who reported on the ups and downs of his travels with a show that consisted of "three moral Bares, a Kangaroo, . . . wax figgers of G. Washington, Gen. Tayler, John Bunyan, Capt. Kidd . . . besides several miscellanyus moral wax statoots of celebrated pirates & murderers."[10] Artemus Ward, that is, was not at all like Charles Farrar Browne. But when in 1863 Clemens began attaching the name "Mark Twain" to his writings, that Mark Twain was, in effect, the same man as the Sam Clemens who wrote the news articles. Only when he began in print and lectures to elaborate with extravagance upon his own experiences did the Mark Twain in the works begin to diverge from the Sam Clemens who had lived the described experience. In life Mark Twain, the author, lecturer, and public figure, led Sam Clemens to increasing public displays of singularity—his famous adoption of white suits in winter as well as other seasons is but one example— and by the close of the century the Sam Clemens who in 1863 had created Mark Twain had turned into him.

Back in Nevada in 1863, those who had known him earlier still called him "Sam." But when he drifted to California and his stories and platform appearances began to widen his audience, friends and acquaintances started to call him "Mark," and people on the San Francisco streets who had never heard of Samuel Clemens recognized his person as that of Mark Twain. As his fame grew in succeeding decades and he took up residence in the East, almost all who knew him personally, like his closest friend, Joseph Twichell, Hartford neighbor and the companion on the travels elaborated in *A Tramp Abroad* (1880), called him "Mark," yet his invaluable literary advisor, William Dean Howells, another close friend, always called him "Clemens." But although Clemens and Twain became the same person in life, the Mark Twain in the books always lingered in maturity well behind the Sam Clemens whose experiences were being imaginatively recalled, so that, for example, although the Clemens who went west in 1861 was an experienced riverboat pilot familiar with the waterfront life of New Orleans and St. Louis, the Twain who goes west in *Roughing It* is, in his want of worldliness, a credulous adolescent.

Publishing constantly in magazines and newspapers, producing books at a steady rate, and quoted widely on all matters—what Mark Twain had to say about any current event was instant newspaper copy and quickly became public lore—he was the most famous American of his day. His international renown exceeded that of statesmen, military heroes, inventors, and the most popular of the day's entertainers. In London and Vienna, police stopped traffic when he wished to cross the street, and American conductors held trains for him if he was late to arrive. In June 1907, Oxford University conferred the degree of Doctor of Letters upon him in company with a prime minister, an archbishop, and a royal prince, but what was equally impressive about his worldwide fame was that when he disembarked from the ship on which he had traveled to England to receive the honor, the stevedores at dockside—who may have been ignorant of the purpose of his visit—nevertheless recognized his person and cheered him because he was Mark Twain. At one of the Oxford banquets held in his honor, the catering manager dressed as a waiter in order to serve the man all of whose books he had read, and, characteristically, when Twain heard of this he drew the sometimes waiter aside for a chat.

Although since Twain's day electronic media and the publicity mills of the entertainment industry have combined to create celebrities on an even wider scale, the fame of such celebrities has within their lifetime lacked the staying power of his because, finally, the countless manifestations of the public's regard for him arose from something deeper than an appreciation of his literary achievement or attraction to the magnetism of celebrity itself— they were expressions of love. Twain himself called his fame "submerged fame." It is, he explained, "the fame that permeates the great crowd of people you never see and never mingle with; people with whom you have no speech, but who read your books and become admirers of your work and have an affection for you."[11] In his description of the way the gatemen in Grand Central Terminal held the train until Twain arrived, William Dean Howells said, they "are proud to know him and lay hold of him, and put him aboard *something* that leaves for Riverdale. . . . they would not let it go without him, if it was the Chicago limited!"[12] We may read "lay hold of him" literally—the working man's touch of affection for a person who, however distinguished he may have been, they also recognized as one of their own. "Printer, pilot, soldier [albeit for three weeks], gold-washer, the child of emigrations [from the Atlantic seaboard to, and within, the West], a pilgrim in another [that of the 'innocents' touristic journey to the Holy Land], a sharer in the flush times, a shaper of the gilded age—he more completely than any other writer, took part in the American experience."[13]

Mark Twain was living in Virginia City and working on the *Enterprise* in 1863 when Artemus Ward came to the region of the Comstock Lode to deliver lectures—Virginia City had a fine new opera house—and, veteran newsman that he was, used the *Enter-prise* office as his headquarters during his stay. The good times he had drinking and storytelling with the local writers led Ward to remain for three weeks, well beyond the dates of his lectures. There Twain and he first met, and they quickly became close friends. The nationally known Ward recognized the great talent of the *Enterprise* reporter whose reputation was as yet local, encouraged him to begin submitting work to eastern magazines, and after his visit wrote back to Twain and his other drinking companions, "I shall always remember Virginia as a bright spot in my existence, as all others must or cannot be, as it were." The bumbling mean-der into a baffling end that makes no sense whatsoever was char-acteristic of Ward's style of bemused humor on the lecture platform where, even as his audience laughed, he kept a straight face, ap-pearing to believe that he was making sense and was ignorant of whatever caused the laughter. Ward closed his letter to his new companions with the seemingly unconnected observation, "Some of the finest intellects in the world have been blunted by liquor."[14] Both the comic unawareness of having become so tangled in one's prose that he has drifted into nonsense, and the reflective, appar-ently anticlimactic, afterthought that has both nothing and yet everything to do with what preceded it, were soon to become fea-tures of Twain's manner. Well beyond Ward, however, he wove such essentially oral storytelling devices into the very fabric of great written prose.

Writing about the all but infinite distance between Twain and the literary comedians of his time, Bernard De Voto said, "Artemus remains merely a fashion of our ancestors, an object of antiquar-ian interest only."[15] But while it is true that Artemus Ward is just about unreadable in this day—the arch misspellings that once provoked laughter are now tiresome in the extreme—De Voto's impatience with literary criticism, which he called a "department of beautiful thinking too insulated for my taste,"[16] perhaps distracted him from noting the very real influence upon Twain of Ward's emphasis upon the guileless voice of a simple-hearted speaker. In one of his lectures, Twain quoted Ward on the slow speed of western railroads: "He once told the conductor the cowcatcher should be at the other end—there the danger lay. 'You can't,' said he, 'overtake a cow, but what's to hinder one walking in the back door and biting the passengers?'"[17] That lovely idiocy points the way for Twain's comic sublime.

Mark Twain moved on from the silver-mining region of Nevada to the gold mines of California and then to newspaper work in San Francisco. When Ward and he met again in that city in 1865, Ward was in the process of gathering a collection of humorous stories for a book. He told Twain to write up the anecdote he had been telling about the frog of one Jim Smiley and send it to Carleton, his publisher, for inclusion in the book. But by the time the manuscript reached New York the book had already gone to press, and Carleton instead offered the story to the editor of the *Saturday Press* where it appeared in the November 18, 1865, issue titled "Jim Smiley and His Jumping Frog." The story was immediately taken up by newspaper after newspaper in every region of the country, and on the basis of this one story the name Mark Twain became known nationwide.

Twain himself did not quite comprehend the extent of his celebrity until after he left California for journalism in New York, and lectured in various cities along his eastward route. He was not as thrilled as might have been expected. "To think," he wrote in a letter of January 20, 1866, "that after writing many an article a man might be excused for thinking tolerably good, those New York people should single out a villainous backwoods sketch to compliment me on!" It was a "squib which would never have been written but to please Artemus Ward."[18]

Even as his fame grew in the following years, Twain would continue to be subject to similar moods of unhappiness about the nature of his literary reputation. When in lecturing on Artemus Ward, for example, he said that amusing as Ward was, "he must not be compared with Holmes or Lowell," he was also indicating a sense of his own inferiority to the two New Englanders. What was the merit of the "Celebrated Jumping Frog of Calaveras County," as it was titled soon after its initial publication, compared with the urbane wit of Holmes's essays? Lowell and Holmes, Twain said, "have a refinement that he [Ward] did not possess, but this does not detract from the great showman's ability to create fun for the millions."[19] It may not detract, but neither does it for Twain place the author who creates fun for the millions in the apparently more desirable position of a "refined" writer. One can guess it was not just Ward he was talking about.

When James Russell Lowell consented to become the founding editor of the *Atlantic Monthly* in 1857, the year Sam Clemens paid a master pilot $500 to train him, Lowell agreed to do so provided he could persuade the great medical pioneer, Dr. Oliver Wendell Holmes, foremost of the Boston wits, to contribute to the magazine. The first issue contained an essay by Holmes, dramatized as the conversation of an erudite and witty Bostonian presiding over the breakfast table of a boardinghouse where the brief responses to his soliloquies by the other boarders allowed him to comment on their comments, and so become the Boswell to his designedly Johnsonian self. The essays that followed in the same vein—nimble yet penetrating—were popular with the new magazine's readers and went a good way toward establishing the *Atlantic* as the urbane voice of literary America, with Boston as its capital. When in 1858 these essays were gathered into a book, *The Autocrat of the Breakfast Table*, young Mark Twain regarded the collection as the single best American work of comic art.

The *Autocrat*'s wittiness now seems too coy and his pellucid prose too self-satisfied for modern tastes, in good part, ironically, because of Mark Twain's subsequent achievement. But the ground of Twain's admiration may still be appreciated. Wide erudition brought to bear on daily trivia yielded a series of pleasing surprises, and when Holmes wrote, "Why can't somebody give us a list of things that everybody thinks and nobody says, and another list of things that everybody says and nobody thinks?" he was describing the theme of many of the surprises his prose could spring.

For all the distance between the Autocrat's seat at the Boston table and Twain's raucous bivouacs, between his richly allusive phrasing and Twain's lively colloquialisms, they shared a tireless concern for the health of language, and, indeed, Twain's may very well have originated in his admiration for Holmes. "People that make puns are like wanton boys that put coppers on the railroad tracks," Holmes wrote. "They amuse themselves and other children but their trick may upset a freight train of conversation for the sake of a battered witticism." Although his articulation of such matters was sharply different, Twain agreed. He learned from Holmes, not with regard to the relatively minor matter of the wretched puerility of punning—he needed no advice there—but with regard to the larger proposition that language is the vehicle of social intercourse, and to trivialize it is to tamper with the medium of human intelligence.[20] None of Twain's uneducated narrators (Huck is a prime example) even at their slangiest do other than advance language's expressive capacity; the damage is done by the educated or pretentious characters who in their inflated locutions detach language from a lived reality.

In 1874 Mark Twain himself finally entered the pages of the *Atlantic*, a significant arrival not only for him but for American literary culture in general. Under William Dean Howells's editorship that register of America's highest literary aspirations crossed the intellectual frontier of Boston to invite writing that reflected the manners of a larger nation. Yet when Holmes later wrote to Twain he praised him for his "frequently quaint and amusing conceits"; he did not call Twain's work literature.[21] For all of Twain's admission into the vestibule of the temple, the New England keepers of the flame still held him at a safe distance from the literary altar, and Twain felt it.

The "villainous backwoods sketch" that, somewhat to his chagrin, began Mark Twain's rise to eminence was also—although Howells was perhaps alone in then suspecting it—the beginning of the end of literate America's taste for humor such as Holmes's. The humor of "The Celebrated Jumping Frog" came out of a frontier narrative tradition, that of the Old Southwest, which was popular among readers of newspapers and comic magazines but only sporadically held the interest of book readers. Sketches in the tradition varied from passingly funny through tediously crude to downright distressing in their appetite for violence, and the wide appeal the "Jumping Frog" exercised on readers of serious literature—as well as the readers of comic papers—was the result of the way it retained the performing essence of an essentially oral, storytelling tradition while transmuting it into carefully crafted prose fiction: cleansing it of its crudeness but not of its vocabulary; simulating its long-windedness without itself being long-winded.

The characteristic humorous tale of the Old Southwest encloses the monologue of an illiterate backwoods speaker, unconscious of how funny he is, within the narrative of a speaker who like the reader is literate. In presenting the colorful tale-teller for our entertainment, the narrator in effect invites us to join him on a social plane well above that of the unsophisticated tale-teller and from that vantage take delight in the earthy vigor of the tale and the unconscious simplicity of the speaker. The best of such tales are verbal equivalents of primitive genre paintings in their depiction of characteristic, albeit exaggerated, frontier scenes.[22] The masterpiece of the tradition is Thomas Bang Thorpe's "The Big Bear of Arkansas," first published in 1841. It begins, "A steamboat on the Mississippi, frequently in making her regular trips, carries between places varying one or two thousand miles apart, and, as these boats advertise to land passengers and freight 'at all intermediate landings,' the heterogeneous character of the passengers of one of those up-country boats can scarcely be imagined by one who has never seen it with his own eyes." The long, compounded, complex, opening sentence provides a literate frame designed to heighten the contrast between the narrator and the backwoods talker who will occupy the picture within it. As the narrator traveling on the steamboat is "busily employed in reading," he is startled by a loud whoop, and Jim Dagget walks into the stateroom. With a bit of prodding from the stateroom's more sophisticated inhabitants he launches into the greatest of all Southwestern monologues, one that will end in a bear-hunting story that is equaled only by William Faulkner's "The Bear." Faulkner, indeed, knew and admired the "Big Bear," saying, "A writer is afraid of a story like that. He's afraid he'll try to rewrite it. A writer has to learn when to run from a story."[23]

Making his way toward the climactic bear hunt, Dagget tells one or another anecdote to illustrate his claim that Arkansas is the "creation state," with glories unmatched elsewhere. Its mosquitoes, to be sure, are enormous, "But mosquitoes is nature, and I never find fault with her. If they ar large, Arkansaw is large, her varmints ar large, her trees ar large, her rivers ar large, and a small mosquito would be of no more use in Arkansaw than preaching in a cane-break." The tale of the hunt itself has the resonating, unarticulated implications of classical myth, but they are, unfortunately, cheapened by the narrator's patronizing return to complete the frame: "it was evident there was some superstitious awe connected with the affair—a feeling common with all 'children of the wood,' when they meet with any thing out of their every day experience." That "awe" arises from Dagget's inarticulate awareness that in hunting the bear he has crossed into the presence of the supernatural, and neither does he deserve nor the reader appreciate the narrator's condescension.

In the force of its mythic content "The Big Bear of Arkansas" compares favorably with anything Twain wrote in that vein, and the figures and rhythmic syntax of the teller's speech approach the heights Twain was to achieve. The all-telling difference, however, that which has elevated the "Jumping Frog" above the "Big Bear" and the conventions of its tradition, is Twain's inspired incorporating of the narrator into the texture of the fiction rather than employing him to keep the reader at a sanitary distance from the monologue. In so doing he converts reported anecdote into seamless story.

The "Jumping Frog" deceptively begins within the conventions of the genteel narrator:

> In compliance with the request of a friend of mine, who wrote me from the East, I called on good-natured, garrulous old Simon Wheeler, and inquired after my friend's friend, *Leonidas W.* Smiley, as requested to do, and I hereunto append the result.

Again we are being led to the ingenuous tale-teller by a literate narrator, his opening sentence even exceeding Thorpe's in its use of Latinate diction and its inclusion of two dependent clauses in its compound syntax. The crucial difference is then unobtrusively introduced in the next two sentences:

> I have a lurking suspicion that *Leonidas W.* Smiley is a myth; that my friend never knew such a personage; and that he only conjectured that if I asked old Wheeler about him, it would remind him of his infamous *Jim* Smiley, and he would go to work and bore me nearly to death with some infernal reminiscences of him as long and tedious as it should be useless to me. If that was his design, it certainly succeeded.

Twain's narrator, that is, unlike those who preceded him in the tradition, has no sense of humor; what will delight us will bore him. The deliberately measured opening sentences, which he believes identify him with the reader, actually separate him, and thus separated he becomes part of the story, not, as he thinks, merely its reporter. Seeking out the tale-teller in order to obtain a prosaic piece of information, he is closed to anything else, however magical it may be. When at the close Wheeler is summoned away and says, "Jest set where you are stranger, and rest easy—I ain't going to be a second," the narrator assumes he has the reader's sympathy when he says, "But by your leave, I did not think that a continuation of the history of the enterprising vagabond *Jim* Smiley would be likely to afford me much information concerning the Rev. *Leonidas W. Smiley*, and so I hurried away." The reader, of course, is left wishing to hear more. There was a yellow-tailed cow yet to be added to the gallery of Andrew Jackson, the fighting dog, and Daniel Webster, the jumping frog, when Wheeler returned, but now, thanks to the narrator's denseness, it will forever remain hidden. The amusing details in the monologue to which he listened impatiently are imbued with the charm of Wheeler's innocent belief in the self-consciousness of animals and his artless assumption that the oddities he describes are part of the usual order of things; the narrator's failure to be charmed, as is the reader, makes him a comic constituent of the story rather than the sober guide to it that he assumes himself to be. In later work Twain was to employ and refine this technique, which reached its apotheosis in the tale of "My Grandfather's Ram" in *Roughing It*. When Jim Blaine, the monologuist in that tale, piles up the incongruous details that provoke so many laughs they soon cease to be separate but flow steadily along as his voice drones on, the narrator becomes vexed at the time he has wasted listening and believes that those who told him that he would enjoy listening to Blaine have played a practical joke on him.

The prank that is the presumed point of the jumping frog story is obvious and not very funny. A stranger, who bets that a frog that is picked up at random can outjump Jim Smiley's celebrated Daniel Webster, surreptitiously weighs Dan'l down with shot and wins his bet. But it is the telling, not the tale, that counts; or, rather, the telling *is* the tale. Wheeler's unflagging belief in the gravity of the zany doings he reports, and the narrator's ponderous inability to find anything funny in what he is hearing, reinforce one another to form a whole. "The Celebrated Jumping Frog of Calaveras

County" is a work of literary art. When Mark Twain, newly arrived in the East and eager for literary recognition there, called his story "a villainous backwoods sketch," he unconsciously duplicated his narrator's misestimation of the tale Simon Wheeler had told him. The "Jumping Frog" was a strong first step toward the kind of authorial fame he desired, although throughout his subsequent career he would be subject to doubts that the writing of humor could ever be equal in importance to books with a graver manner—even mediocre ones.

> Upon the glazen shelves kept watch
> —Matthew and Waldo, guardians of the faith,
> The army of unalterable law.

So runs T. S. Eliot's amused description of the moral tone of high Boston culture in the latter half of the nineteenth century. And although in his lecture tours Waldo Emerson did come to some sense of another culture and the approaching need for writers to address it in terms different from his, Matthew Arnold steadfastly maintained that the sober high ground was the site of civilization itself. His young admirer, Henry James, wrote, "Mr. Arnold's supreme virtue is that he speaks of things seriously, or in other words, that he is not offensively clever."[24]

When Arnold visited Boston on his 1883 lecture tour to America, he called on William Dean Howells and was told by Mrs. Howells that her husband was in Hartford visiting Mark Twain. This surprised him. "But he doesn't like *that* sort of thing, does he?" he asked her. Later in the tour when Arnold visited Hartford, he met Twain at a reception and went with other guests to dinner at his home. There the steady current of Twain's talk kept the table in constant laughter and led Arnold to ask another guest, "And is he *never* serious?"[25]

In 1886 during another lecture tour in America, Arnold gathered the impressions he published as *Civilization in the United States* (1888). In that book he spoke of the humor of Mark Twain as an expression of the Philistinism of people of "his type." "Childish and half-savage minds," he said, "are not moved except by very elementary narratives composed without art, in which burlesque and melodrama, vulgarity and eccentricity, are combined in strong doses."[26] The American addiction to the "funny man" is a "national misfortune,"[27] operating as it does to inhibit distinction and leave Americans satisfied with the average or worse in their culture as well as in their politics.

It was easier then, as it is now, for Americans to become outraged at these remarks than to acknowledge the conditions that gave rise to them. There *was* a national habit of brag that drowned out intelligent social criticism and a glorification of the "average man" that made difficult individual attempts to excel. Indeed, excellence itself was deemed a good thing only if, self-contradictorily, everyone could achieve it. A constructive reply to Arnold's arguments was certainly possible, but the outraged responses they drew more often exemplified his contentions about the low level of American culture than refuted them.

Mark Twain, to be sure, was among those who took issue with Arnold. After all, he had been singled out by name as well as included in the general scorn for the "funny man." But his public refutation, most prominently in his 1892 novel, *The American Claimant*, was not so encompassing nor so persuasive as the argument he intended to rebut. Defending American newspapers against Arnold's charge that they pandered to the unintelligence of the masses, Twain insisted that the very irreverence of American journalism was its strength. English journals keep the public eye fixed on the sacredness of the throne, the hereditary nobility, and the established church, he said, and thus collude in the social injustice visited upon the English working man, while, on the other hand, American newspapers stand guard over the common man's liberties. But his claim cannot persuade those who remember that Twain himself lampooned the petty vindictiveness and execrable language of small-town newspapers, the very journals that he now was maintaining were in touch with the democratic values he alleged they represented. In a talk he gave in 1872 he had said, "The more newspapers the worse morals. . . . We *ought* to look upon the establishment of a newspaper of the average pattern in a virtuous village as a calamity."[28]

By switching the argument to politics—pitting the American social order against the British—Twain was circumventing Arnold's central contentions about the sorry state of American civilization, and, more specifically, of American literature. He evaded that issue, one suspects, because even though he resented Arnold's citing of the "funny man" as a prime example of what was wrong with American literature, deeper in his consciousness he feared that, finally, his achievement was, indeed, sub-literary.

When Arnold's book appeared in 1888, Mark Twain was at the height of his form. He had published two story collections, four travel books, among them *The Innocents Abroad* (1869), which to this day remains the most popular travel book ever written by an American, and four novels, including *Tom Sawyer* (1876) and the indestructible masterpiece *Huckleberry Finn* (1884). One after another, his lecture tours had been triumphantly popular and profitable, and his speeches at commemorative dinners and public ceremonies were enthusiastically quoted in the newspapers. Did you hear what Mark Twain said about one or another event or person was a part of everyday conversation. Indeed, so newsworthy were the remarks in his talks that he was concerned that the instant coverage would prevent him from repeating material he wanted to use more than once before putting it into print. As his popularity grew he reversed the usual arrangement between publisher and author by taking the expenses of publishing his books upon himself and paying the publisher a percentage for printing them, and then, in 1884, established his own publishing firm, Charles L. Webster and Company, which published *Huckleberry Finn* in the following year. He also made the same reversal of proprietorship for his platform tour with George Washington Cable in 1884, hiring someone to manage the tour but himself being its owner. Paying Cable the considerable fee of $450 a week plus expenses, he nevertheless came out with a handsome profit. The grandiose Hartford mansion into which he moved in 1870 proclaimed his glorious arrival at international celebrity and his unabashed love of display—Tom Sawyer come into his own—and for the next twenty years in his study there, he produced the best work of his career. Yet the anxiety about his stature, expressed in his comment about the "villainous backwoods sketch" twenty years before Matthew Arnold took public note of him, continued to stalk him through the period of his great success.

Twain could speak forcibly in defense of humor as a literary mode equal to graver modes and, in its effects, just as serious. "There are those who say a novel should be a work of art solely, and you must not preach in it, you must not teach in it. That may be true as regard novels but it is not true as regards humor," he said. "Humor must not professedly teach, and it must not professedly preach, but it must do both if it would live forever."[29]

When he was awarded an honorary Master of Arts degree by Yale in 1888, the year of Arnold's *Civilization in the United States*, Twain began his letter of acceptance with a jest—"To be made a master of arts by your venerable college is an event of large size to me, and a distinction which gratifies me as much as if I deserved it"—then went on to say that a friendly word was needed after Arnold's rebuke of the guild of "funny men." "Ours is a useful trade, a worthy calling, that with all its frivolity . . . has one serious purpose, one aim, one specialty, and it is constant to it—the deriding of shams, the exposure of pretentious falsities, the laughing of stupid superstitions out of existence, and whoso is by instinct engaged in this sort of warfare is . . . the natural friend of human rights and human liberties."[30]

The record of his ten books and many stories, sketches, and speeches to that date fully supported his large claim about the "serious purpose" of humor, and his subsequent career, which increasingly turned from fictions to essays that directly addressed political knavery at home and racist imperialism abroad, continued to speak for human rights and human liberties. Understandably, then, the vexation Twain said his wife felt at the low regard in which some held his work, "the thing that gravels her is that I am so persistently glorified as a mere buffoon, as if that entirely covered my case—which she denies with venom,"[31] was a vexation and a venom that he shared. Yet the record also shows that, less articulately, Twain did suspect that the critics had valid reasons to regard his achievement as sub-literary: his mode was humorous with frequent swerving into burlesque, and his books were not published by trade publishers and sold in bookstores as were the works of the most respected authors but were published by subscription and sold by door-to-door canvassers.

Subscription publishing had had an honorable history. A long list of great works—such as editions of Shakespeare's plays or Johnson's dictionary—awaited the financial commitment of wealthy and socially distinguished patrons before the printer-bookseller could afford to proceed with their publication. But by the mid-nineteenth century, especially in the United States, subscription publishers aimed at another kind of patron, the working householder, and employed door-to-door canvassers to seek him out. Although literacy was common among lower- as well as upper-income families, the greater part of the population was scattered over the continent at a distance from the relatively few urban centers that could support bookstores; subscription publishers brought their books to the consumer rather than requiring him to come to them. The canvassers carried a portfolio with sample pages, sample illustrations, and a range of bindings from which the subscriber could choose, and not until a sufficient number of purchasers signed up did the actual printing of the book commence. Subscription publishers did not hesitate to proclaim that their going directly to the people was an enterprise more suitable for a democratic population than was the faintly elitist practice of trade publishers who required readers to come to them.

Nevertheless, through the nineteenth century America's most respected authors, such as Emerson, Longfellow, Hawthorne, Henry James, and Howells were published by trade houses, and magazines and newspapers ordinarily reviewed only trade books. There was something distinctly vulgar about associating a work that had pretensions to literary merit with a traveling salesman trained in the techniques of getting his or her foot in the door. "Women who can devote time to the work often make the best of canvassers,"[32] said an advertisement soliciting book agents for the American Publishing Company, the publisher of Mark Twain's first books.

Because the canvassers called upon essentially rural and religious households, subscription books tilted heavily toward spiritual uplift, while travels, especially to biblical sites, were also prominent. The Civil War, however, was the most popular of all subscription subjects, and publishers not only supplied such books but shrewdly sought out veterans, especially those who had been wounded, to serve as agents—how could an open door be denied them? In keeping with the fact that the average household that purchased such books purchased perhaps only one or two books a year, the purchaser had to be guaranteed his money's worth in size and visual appeal every bit as much as in content. Most subscription books ran to at least six hundred pages, and all were heavily illustrated. They were designed to be not just reading matter but, like the horsehair sofa or the chromo on the wall, an integral part of the material furnishings of the sitting room. When, after publishing some half-dozen books with the American Publishing Company, Twain founded the Charles L. Webster Company, that, too, was a subscription house; *Huckleberry Finn* was the first of his books to be published by the firm. A pamphlet issued by the company to its canvassers instructed them not to show the prospectus until they were in the door, to keep talking so that there was no chance for an objection to be raised, never to say "dollars" or "cents" but rather just "three fifty," to flatter the prospective customer, and, above all to work themselves up to love the book and love to talk about it.

Those who frequented bookstores where Twain's books were not available could obtain them by writing to the publisher, while those remote from stores could order them from the agents who had brought the books to their attention. The profits consequent upon this expansion of his public clearly justified his adherence to subscription publication. Yet his association with it also differentiated him from the recognized literary leaders whose books were issued by trade publishers. This contributed to the chafing sense of inferiority that flared up from time to time and seems finally to have eased only three years before his death, when the soothing balm was applied by Oxford University. Before then, remarks such as the following—sent to the British critic Andrew Lang—reveal in their overinsistence on not really wanting to be regarded as cultured an uneasy if aggressive acceptance of a lower status than he desired or than, one may assert, he deserved: "I have never tried, in even one single little instance, to help cultivate the cultivated classes. I was not equipped for it either by native gifts or training. And I never had any ambition in that direction, but always hunted for bigger game—the masses."[33]

To be sure he fetched that game. But his stature in his day as in ours arises from his drawing readers of all sorts or levels of literary sophistication into his audience. He was admired by British contemporaries such as Thomas Hardy, Rudyard Kipling, George Bernard Shaw, and Robert Louis Stevenson—peace be to Matthew Arnold!—as well as by his American contemporaries, while a list of twentieth-century writers who praise his work would stretch from William Faulkner and Ernest Hemingway to Arthur Miller and Toni Morrison; indeed, include just about all authors of note. In a period in which the novel-reading public was predominantly female, he was read by men who ordinarily read newspapers or ledgers but not books. And those who read him reread him with remarkable frequency. A number of his works centered on young people, and while he was occasionally puzzled as to whether to market them as children's or as adult's literature, they effortlessly succeeded in attracting both audiences. Humor is finely tied to the culture in which it is produced and, notoriously, turns flat when carried abroad, but Twain's crossed borders, in the original or in translation, with remarkable ease—the Maharajah of Bikanir as well as the Oxford caterer sought his acquaintance— and for all the self-evident talk of the quintessentially American nature of his work, beyond any other American author Mark Twain became the possession of the world.

Two

TOURIST

M ARK T WAIN ACHIEVED HIS FIRST GREAT LITERARY SUCCESS, AND IT was enormous, with the publication in 1869 of *The Innocents Abroad*, a travel book that, in effect, upended the genre.[1] Previous to its appearance, travel writers had typically offered serious instruction through a mixture of weighty objective descriptions and earnest subjective impressions. Far from innocent of instructive intent, *Innocents Abroad* was, nevertheless, blithesome and satiric. Throughout its 651-page length Twain demonstrated that his celebrated jumping frog story had not been a novelty but was the opening salvo in the campaign of a major literary figure.

Years later, after he had become a husband and father and after he had his fill of being a traveling lecturer, Twain would curse the idea of having to set out on further journeys, yet he returned time and again to the travel book and thus to the travel it required. In advance of departure he could contract to supply letters to newspapers, and upon his return contract again to edit and assemble them for publication in book form. None of his other writings could so assure him of profits before he even set pen to paper. What is more, even the discomforts of travel provided ready-made subject matter for a humorist.

Even though he came to detest travel itself, there was also sound literary reason for Twain's attraction to travel writing. He was a master at revealing character through dialogue and gesture, and at capturing in the printed marks on the page the pitch and stress of the spoken American language—to read his work is to hear it. He was not, however, an accomplished maker of extended plots but was at his best in short pieces or in incidents within his novels, while the plots of the novels as a whole were vulnerable to his propensity to wander from the path before him into the byways of burlesque, one-line jokes, and occasional sentimentality. Rather than weaving incidents into the complex network of cause and effect that is a plot, Twain managed a sequence of events most tellingly when they reflected his imagination's meanderings—as one thing led him to another they were associated with in his mind—a method better suited to travel reports than to fiction. His first novel, *The Gilded Age* (1873), was written collaboratively with Charles Dudley Warner, as if consistency of tone and a necessary connection between what happened and what followed was less important than the presentation of a series of lively episodes; more than once later in his career he attempted to interest other writers in contributing to a novel in which each would write a chapter. Even *Huckleberry Finn*, that enduring monument of American art, suffers in its concluding chapters from Twain's constitutional inability to pass up a comic opportunity when it occurred to him, regardless of its thematic incoherence.

Traveling, however, by its very nature is loosely joined. A journey's serial progress from place to place supplied him with a frame rather than a form, and he could put into this frame other scenes and other times as the memory of them was prompted by the sight before him. The wonderful yarn of Jim Baker and the blue jays in the California Sierra in *A Tramp Abroad* (1880), for example, was called up when, during a stroll in a German wood, he heard the ravens croaking. Such imaginative drifting from the path and back to it, potentially damaging in a novel, enriched rather than detracted from the narrative of his travels.

Mark Twain was thirty-one when he arrived in New York somewhat irked to find his reputation that of a backwoods humorist. For the past five-and-one-half years he had lived on the Pacific slopes, first as a miner, then, with increasing success, as a journalist and lecturer. He had reported on the doings of the Nevada legislature with reasonable accuracy and a good deal of wit, and had occasionally reported to eastern journals on one or another West Coast event, but neither of those assignments could have been expected to gain him national attention.

Most likely he regarded his reports from the Sandwich (Hawaiian) Islands as his best work. In 1866 he had traveled to Hawaii from San Francisco as correspondent for the *Sacramento Union* and, upon his return to San Francisco, initiated his career as a platform performer when he announced a lecture on the topic of the Sandwich Islands (dress circle one dollar, family circle fifty cents) in which he mingled the factual with the facetious. The poster announcing his lecture closed with the notice, "Trouble to begin at 8 o'clock," and so extensively did this jesting line spread that, a half year later, he saw it scrawled on the walls of a New York jail where it meant something much more sobering.[2]

During his eastward journey to New York Twain delivered the Sandwich Island lecture in St. Louis, where a local newspaper commented that "He succeeded in doing what we have seen Emerson and other literary men fail in attempting—he interested and amused a large and promiscuous audience."[3] But his Hawaiian letters to the *Union* did not appear in book form until 1872, when, finding himself some 150 pages short of the 600-page minimum for subscription books, he appended them in revised form to the account of his life in Nevada and California that formed the main body of *Roughing It*. However much it may have irked him at the time of his 1867 arrival in New York, the "Jumping Frog" was his main claim to fame.

From New York Twain reported back to the *Alta California* on a range of lively topics: omnibuses, theatrical presentations, women's fashions, crowded streets, the Russian Bath, and Barnum's Museum among them. He attended Anna Dickinson's feminist lecture, which was, he said, "worth listening to," and, a skilled ironist himself, described with delight her response to a male heckler who had asked, "Would you have *all* women strong-minded?" "No," she said, "God forbid that the millions of men of your calibre that cumber the earth should be doomed to travel its weary ways unmated."[4] At the other extreme he described in all permissible detail the scandalously unclad women in *The Black Crook*, the spectacle that first brought to the American stage what came to be known as the "girlie show." "Bare-legged girls hanging in flower baskets . . . nothing but a wilderness of girls—stacked up, pile on pile, away aloft to the dome of the theatre, diminishing in size and clothing." It touches, he said "my missionary instinct."[5] On Sundays he attended different churches in order to hear Henry Ward Beecher and other luminaries of the New York pulpit preach, and he reported on them as performers. Their platform styles rather than the content of their sermons were what interested him. With his own lecture career underway he seems to have observed them as would a budding professional alert to pick up pointers.

Some twenty-five years later, in sharp disagreement with historical Christianity, Twain was to formulate his own religious philosophy, both explicitly in essays such as "What Is Man?" and implicitly in fictions such as *A Connecticut Yankee in King Arthur's Court*. But from the very start of his literary career through to his later years of rage at the effects of Christian missions upon native populations, he was attracted to the companionship of ministers. From the West the young journalist wrote his mother about his friendship with one or another preacher, and although such news was certainly designed to ease her anxiety about her notoriously irreligious son, it was also true. Years later in Hartford the famous writer's closest friend was the Reverend Joseph Twichell, a Congregational minister, and ministers were often on the list of dinner guests at his home. Twain's companion and biographer, Albert Bigelow Paine, said that Twain had a natural leaning toward ministers of the Gospel despite his unorthodoxy and his hatred of cant and the curtailment of liberty, and that they liked him. He attributed this seemingly paradoxical circumstance to a sympathy for mankind that Twain shared with the ministry. While this was doubtless so, however, there was another, more critical, dimension to this paradoxical relationship. Ministers were those members of the literate or cultured population of nineteenth-century America who, in the practice of their profession, had to learn to adapt their relatively superior learning to the understanding of a broader population even while continuing to engage the better-read. Twain was an uneducated writer, in the sense of formal schooling, who, in the practice of his profession, aimed to reach beyond those with limited educational experience (like his own) to a more learned readership even while retaining his broader base. The ministers and Twain met, as it were, on the popular ground that each approached from a different direction, and they intrigued one another, especially so since both placed a heavy reliance on speech. When preparing their sermons, preachers had to write what would be spoken, while Twain, when writing his stories, sought to bring the illusion of speaking to what would be printed.

The middle ground toward which each moved is dramatized with broad comic exaggeration in *Roughing It* when the rough-hewn miner, Scotty Briggs, calls on a minister, described by Twain as a "pale theological student," in order to make arrangements for the funeral of his friend Buck Fanshaw. He begins the interview by asking "Are you the duck that runs the gospel-mill next door?" After some verbal maneuvering the baffled minister manages to understand the question, and when he answers that he is "the spiritual adviser of the little company of believers whose sanctuary adjoins these premises," it is Scotty's turn to struggle to comprehend. But eventually, after extended wrestling with their opposed vocabularies, they arrived at an agreement, and the funeral that followed was judged a great success. The minister had pleased an assemblage of Nevada miners, and, soon after, Scotty became a member of his congregation.

In the letters to the *Union* from Hawaii and those to the *Alta California* from New York Twain addressed a western and predominantly male audience, both in actual fact and also in the rhetoric he employed. A remark he made about "greasers" in a Hawaiian letter, for example, or, in the New York letters, remarks he made about "nigs" and the actress Ada Menken's relationship with Alexander Dumas, who, he pointedly reminded his readers, was a mulatto, are uncomfortably raw indications of the kind of readership whose prejudices he shared at that stage of his career. More broadly, both the topics he chose for the New York letters and the posture of an amused if admittedly provincial outsider he struck when reporting on them—in his treatment, New York was almost as foreign as Hawaii—emphasized his identity with the simplicities of the westerner. Yet even as he asserted the superiority of horse sense over cultural pretension, he conveyed an edgy awareness of there being values beyond his reach. Of the exhibition at the Academy of Design he said, "I know I ought to have admired that picture by one of the old masters, where six bearded faces without any bodies to them were glaring out of Egyptian darkness and glowering upon a naked infant that was not built like any infant that ever I saw, nor colored like it either. I am glad the old masters are all dead, and I only wish they had died sooner."[6] With such a proclamation he was readying himself for a visit to the lands of the old masters and the regions of the Bible.

Contracted to supply fifty-eight letters to the *Alta California* and a few to New York newspapers, Mark Twain sailed from New York in June 1867 upon an excursion to Europe and the Holy Land. The letters he wrote continued to trumpet his unabashed provincialism, and the instant and staggeringly large success of *The Innocents Abroad*, the book he made from these letters at the suggestion of the subscription publisher Elisha Bliss of the American Publishing Company, attested to the joy an enormous population felt at no longer having to pretend to appreciate what they did not like or understand—simply because school teachers and pontificating travel writers had shamed them into doing so. It was, after all, acceptable to laugh at the pieties of high culture, even though, to be sure, to do so one had also to laugh at oneself. Twain was a master at both.

Originating among members of Henry Ward Beecher's Pilgrim Church, the leisurely, six-month excursion to Europe and the Holy Land that he joined was made in a ship exclusively devoted to that purpose—no venture in group tourism on so extended a scale had ever before been undertaken. The itinerary was laid out in advance, and Twain embarked upon it because everything had been prepared for him. He did not know the language of any country he visited, and his foreign acquaintanceship was limited to guides, hoteliers, waiters, and shopkeepers. At no point did he pretend otherwise or wish to alter his condition—to imagine he was a traveler rather than a tourist—because he brilliantly perceived that the originality of his work, compared with other books of travel, would reside in his paying closer attention to the tourist experience and to tourists themselves than to the places visited. *Innocents Abroad* is a book about the comic adventures of a group of tourists, more than it is about the places they visit. They are, indeed, innocents abroad, clueless as to where to go and how to react except as steered by guides and prompted by travel books, and they are indeed fit subjects for humor.

"I make small pretence of showing any one how he *ought* to look at objects of interest beyond the seas," Twain wrote at the beginning of the book. Rather, he suggests to the reader how *he* would see Europe and the Near East if he looked with his own eyes rather than those of previous travelers; if, that is, he swept away the patina of worshipful associations one or another site had acquired from commentators and looked at what was actually before him. Twain's comments aimed at a readership surfeited with travel accounts that emphasized what their own culture lacked by comparison, and they sometimes appear outrageous as they play to the prejudicial resentments of the American reader: Arabs are filthy, squalid, and superstitious; Italians are superstitious, poverty-stricken, and worthless; Portuguese are slow, poor, shiftless, and lazy, and so forth. Yet, at the same time, the reader is always aware that in offering these observations, and so implicitly endorsing them, Twain is also consciously reflecting the shortcomings of an American outlook that is wedded to material achievement as the defining mark of merit. Still, it must also be admitted that there was— and for some may still remain—a streak of readerly pleasure to be experienced from participating silently in incorrect attitudes that one publicly holds to be abhorrent.

The great riches of *Innocents Abroad*, however, reside in the many humorous incidents in which the tourists involve themselves—the blunders they make and the bedevilment they visit upon their guides—and in Twain's stout insistence on reporting what he sees rather than what guide books and travel literature tell him he is seeing. There is, to be sure, a trace of iconoclasm for its own sake in this, but if Twain lacks the training to judge aesthetically, he is stalwart in defending the political outlook that hampers his appreciation of many of the art objects he sees: "My friends abuse me because I am a little prejudiced against the old masters—because I fail sometimes to see the beauty that is in their production," he says. "I can not help but see it, now and then, but I keep on protesting against the groveling spirit that could persuade those masters to prostitute their noble talents to such monsters as the French, Venetian and Florentine Princes of two and three hundred years ago, all the same." Whatever the shortcomings of his aesthetic sensibility, his reaction carries the doughty strain of republicanism that can be viewed, for example, in John Adams's remark to Jefferson that "Every one of the fine Arts from the earliest times have been enlisted in the service of Superstition and Despotism."[7] Twain, too, had patrons, and he could identify them almost as precisely as could a painter employed by a nobleman—because his book was sold by subscription. If his ignorance of art spoke for these patrons so also did the moral offense he took at the sight of impoverished peoples, the political discomfort he felt before artifacts that were commissioned for the gratification of oligarchs, and the trust he placed in humor as a suitable vehicle for the conveyance of these feelings.

Following up on the great success of *Innocents Abroad*, Elisha Bliss asked Twain for an account of his western experiences. Twain started on it in 1870, and *Roughing It* was published by Bliss's American Publishing Company in 1872. Although in the years following publication it did not match the sensational sales record of *Innocents Abroad*, it was, nevertheless, a popular success and, as a literary work, is clearly superior to its predecessor. Since Twain's day it has been far more frequently reprinted. Its picture of the American West in the boom times that followed the gold rush and the unearthing of the Comstock Lode continues to be the classic portrait of that era, and its comic episodes—the purchase of the genuine Mexican plug, the great landslide case, Buck Fanshaw's funeral, the cat who didn't like quartz mining, or Jim Blaine's grandfather's ram—are fresh at each rereading because, unlike humor that builds toward a comic climax and then dissolves as does a joke once the punch line is delivered, the pleasure they provide is embedded in the telling.

Although *Roughing It,* too, is largely episodic and often follows the path of associations rather than the track of travel, it has a theme that underlies its separate scenes and provides a unity lacking in *Innocents Abroad.* That theme is the arrival at maturity of the bumptious young fool who piled into the stagecoach at St. Joseph and journeyed across the continent to Fort Laramie, South Pass, Salt Lake City, Carson City, and the California gold fields finally to emerge as a master storyteller. The tale is told retrospectively—each scene in *Innocents Abroad* unfolded without knowledge of what would occur during the following day—and the difference between the mature author and the youthful subject he makes of himself enhances the reader's experience.

Shortly into their westward journey—Twain is accompanied by his brother Orion—they encounter alkali water in the road. It "excited us," he says, "as much as any wonder we had come upon yet, and I know we felt very complacent and conceited, and better satisfied with life after we had added it to your list of things which *we* had seen and some other people had not." For him, seeing something new or different was not so much of educational as it was of social value. This pleasure in travel derived from the anticipated envy it will arouse in others is prominent in *Innocents Abroad* and recurs with frequency in Twain's fiction; for Tom Sawyer to be famous *and* to be envied are one and the same. But the author of *Roughing It* is wiser than his younger self and adds to his account of alkali water, "In a small way we were the same sort of simpletons as those who climb unnecessarily the perilous peaks of Mont Blanc and the Matterhorn, and derive no pleasure from it except the reflection that it isn't a common experience." He thus alerts himself to guard against such pettiness in reporting on his travels even as he recognizes that trait in the immature self who traveled. He thus also criticizes travel writers who seek out uncommon paths only because they are uncommon (Twain would certainly take a scathing view of those adventurers who today set off on uncommon travels only when accompanied by a camera crew).

"Truly, 'seeing is believing,'" he writes, "and many a man lives a long life through *thinking* he believes certain universally received and well established things, and yet never suspects that if he were confronted by those things once, he would discover that he did not *really* believe them before, but only thought he believed them." Such unseating of the familiar and recentering of belief is the honest reward of travel.

Some sixty hours out of St. Joseph the travelers see their first coyote. He is homely and scrawny with ribs showing through his coarse hair; everything about him seems apologetic. If, however, you start a swift-footed dog after him, writes Twain, you will see the coyote's gentle lope keep him ahead of the hot pursuit of the dog. "The dog is only a short twenty feet behind . . . and to save the soul of him he cannot understand why it is that he cannot get perceptibly closer." The coyote glides along and "never pants or sweats or ceases to smile," and the straining dog, beginning to tire, notices that the coyote actually has to slacken speed to keep from running away from him. This so infuriates the dog that he makes one last strenuous effort, draws within six feet of the coyote, and then, in the next instant, finds himself alone "in the midst of a vast solitude." The coyote, tiring of the game, has zoomed away. Those who have completed *Roughing It* may turn back to that early description and recognize it as a parable. The trim town dog confident in his superiority to a coarse environment is the Mark Twain who left for the West; the sly coyote masking his artfulness behind apparent simpleness is the Mark Twain who returned from there to write about him.

The sales of *Tom Sawyer* (1876), his second novel but the first that he had written without a collaborator, were disappointing, and Twain returned to the travel narrative in order to regain his original audience. *A Tramp Abroad* (1880) succeeded in doing that, but today it seems the least rewarding of his travel writings. His uneasiness, indeed boredom, with the German and Swiss journeys that he undertook as material for the book bleeds through its cheerful surface. There is a good deal of padding as extended passages from other works, for example, a disquisition on glaciers, are inserted into his text, and although there are some striking, original sketches, such as the Jim Baker blue jay story, there are also extended sketches that strain at comedy without attaining it. A prime example is his description of heading a 198-man expedition up the "perilous" route from Zermatt to Riffleberg, actually an easy climb, as a parody of the literature of adventure. Not very funny to begin with, it goes on and on.

At a performance of Wagner's *Lohengrin* Twain disliked the fact that there was not a distinct series of set pieces, but, rather, that musical motifs flowed throughout. And of a Mannheim performance of *King Lear* he wrote, "It is a pain to me to this day, to remember how that old German Lear raged and wept and howled around the stage, with never a response from that hushed house, never a single outburst till the act ended." He preferred the eruptive American audiences, and he keyed his writings as well as his platform performances to bringing out a series of immediate responses rather than building toward a unified effect.

Writing to Howells in January 1879, Twain said, "I wish I *could* give those sharp satires on European life which you mention, but of course a man can't write successful satire except he be in a calm judicial good humor—whereas I *hate* travel, & I *hate* hotels, & I *hate* the opera, & I *hate* the Old Masters—in truth I don't ever seem to be enough in a good humor with anything to *satirize* it; no, I want to stand up before it & *curse* it & foam at the mouth— or take a club & pound it to rags and pulp."[8] The paper pages of *A Tramp Abroad* are the rag and pulp into which Twain pounded his travels. The appendices on German journalism and especially the German language—a sustained comic masterpiece—are superior to any unit of the same length within the text proper.

"Old Times on the Mississippi," Mark Twain's version of his training and career as a riverboat pilot, appeared in seven sketches published in the *Atlantic Monthly* from January to August 1875. No *Atlantic* writer received the same high fees as did Twain, and no reader of "Old Times," then or now, would disagree that he had earned that financial respect, even though the sketches did not measurably affect the magazine's sales because of immediate and widespread newspaper reprinting—there was even a Canadian reprinting in book form—in a day of reckless disregard for copyright. From his desk at the *Atlantic* Howells had often responded generously to Twain's request for critical advice on one or another piece he had written, even if it wasn't destined for his magazine, often counseling restraint and excisions. But as the "Old

Times" sketches began to run, he wrote Twain urging, "Every word is interesting, and don't you drop the series till you've got every bit of anecdote and reminiscences into it."[9] So energized was Twain by the writing and reception of these elaborated memories of his life on the river that he decided to make a trip back to the Mississippi in order to gather material to add to "Old Times" so as to make the whole into a book. The journey would also enable him to utilize the comfortable frame of a travel book.

"Old Times," like *Roughing It*, had portrayed a green Mark Twain arriving at maturity. Those seven *Atlantic* sketches formed twelve of the forty-one chapters of *Life on the Mississippi* (1883), establishing the motive for the travel back to the river. Once those travels are under way, Twain, as would be expected, digresses frequently, but unlike the byways visited in earlier travel books, these digressions are not comic anecdotes. They are, rather, the historical, social, and cultural observations of a deeply moved yet acutely analytical returning son. The eye that once registered the broad differences between Americans and foreigners now more finely focuses upon regional differences. And it is not so much the difference between past and present that concerns the returning native as it is the debilitating persistence of the past.

Moving toward the river by rail, Twain notices a steady diminution in the attractiveness of people and attributes it not to apparel but to the coarseness of their mental outlook. The unattractive habit of wearing goatees without a moustache, which he notes to be the fashion as he moves farther into the hinterlands, is, he says, "accompanied by an iron-clad belief in Adam and the biblical history of creation." Throughout the narrative that follows he skillfully renders the details of a social landscape so that they signify an entire way of life, the technique reaching its zenith in a chapter titled "The House Beautiful." It begins, "Every town and village along that vast stretch of double river-frontage had a best dwelling, finest dwelling mansion," and then, after viewing the facade, he enters the door. In a paragraph that runs for more than four pages Twain provides an unrivaled anatomy of the opinions, sentiments, aspirations, and sorrows of the residents in that vast region simply by passing the reader's eye over one after another of the furnishings of the house: planed wood floors, ingrain carpets, the scenes in the framed lithographs, airtight stove, closed fireplace, two shells—the Lord's Prayer carved on one, portrait of Washington on another (missing the mouth), the crayon drawings of the young ladies of the house, the titles of the books arranged on the center table with a cast-iron exactness, and so on through a range of precisely observed actualizing details to the concluding observation, "not a bathroom in the house; and no visitor likely to come along who had seen one."

The intelligence of such observations comes from the twin perspectives of a two-decades absence from once-familiar territory and a relative cosmopolitanism acquired from foreign travel and residence in the East. There is nostalgia—for the departed steamboats replaced by the railroad, for example—but not sentimentalizing a lingering affection for what once was but a disdain for the attachment to false principles, religious and romantic, that not having been outgrown continue to stunt society. In the North, he says, the Civil War is mentioned in social conversation rather infrequently, but in the South it is the great topic of conversation. That is understandable because *all* southerners were, one way or another, in the war, and the war provided such a range of experiences that it is the measure of any other experience that might come up in conversation. Yet, in comparison, the French Revolution for all the crimes committed did get rid of the sway of the church and the situating of birth above merit, while the postwar South continues its attachment to the sham aristocratic values of its vanished prewar society.

At the conclusion of his journey Twain travels back up the river from New Orleans, continuing north past St. Louis. Of the residents of the upper-river region he writes, "This is an independent race who think for themselves, and who are competent to do it, because they are educated and enlightened; they read; they keep abreast in their land with a school, a college, a library, and a newspaper; and they live under law. Solicitude for the future of a race like this is not in order." Such solicitude, however, is the strain of his discerning contemplation of southern society along the Mississippi in 1882.

After completing *Life on the Mississippi* Twain returned refreshed to complete the manuscript of a novel that had long remained stalled on his desk. *Huckleberry Finn* was completed in 1884. That novel, like *Tom Sawyer*, published nine years before, was concerned with a boy and his life on the banks of the Mississippi in the prewar era. But unlike the viewpoint of *Tom Sawyer*, the steady gaze of *Huckleberry Finn*'s youthful narrator contemplated a world beyond that of boyish adventures, one in which violence erupted from love and fraud preyed upon sorrow, a world in which the reality of slavery was so omnipresent that its blatant inhumanity passed unnoticed among the most decent of citizens. *Tom Sawyer*, told by a third-person narrator, is a loving recall of the joys and anxieties of boyhood, rightfully uncomplicated by adult concerns, whereas *Huckleberry Finn*, told by a boy, is a many-sided, critical portrait of an entire civilization. Although both are set in the time of Twain's boyhood in Hannibal, the profounder implications of *Huckleberry Finn* derive from the adult's return to his past, chronicled in *Life on the Mississippi*. *Tom Sawyer* is a memory; *Huckleberry Finn* a recognition.

In the thirteen years preceding *A Tramp Abroad*, Twain had published nine books: five were collections drawn from the wealth of stories and sketches that had appeared in magazines; two, *The Gilded Age* (in collaboration with Charles Dudley Warner) and *Tom Sawyer*, were novels; and two, *The Innocents Abroad* and *Roughing It*, were travel books. Writing of his 1879 return from Europe in the final pages of *A Tramp Abroad*, he said, "I was glad to get home—immeasurably glad; so glad, in fact, that it did not seem possible anything could ever get me out of the country again." For the next fifteen years nothing did, and the range and size of his literary output were extraordinary: one travel book, *Life on the Mississippi* (1883); five novels, *The Prince and the Pauper* (1882), *The American Claimant* (1882), *The Adventures of Huckleberry Finn* (1884), *A Connecticut Yankee in King Arthur's Court* (1889), and *Pudd'nhead Wilson* (1894)—he wrote no novels after this period—and a steady stream of shorter works, a great number of which were gathered into books. Each day, it seemed, added to his fame and his enjoyment. No dinner speaker was more sought after, and so many were the worthy causes to which he responded that eventually he would agree to appear only after dinner had been consumed and preliminary speakers had concluded. Still, when he did arrive he frequently found, to his exasperation, that the earlier speakers were grinding on beyond their allotted time.

Although his literary earnings would have been adequate to support his family in the bounteous life centered in their Hartford mansion, Twain's investments in his own failing publishing house, together with his copious monetary support for the development of an automatic typesetter that promised astronomical profits if only *one* more costly adjustment could be paid for, then just one *other*, and then maybe *another*, ad infinitum, brought financial ruin. In 1895, after the application of one after another remedy to his failing situation, he was forced into bankruptcy. His heady optimism about the economic miracle that was industrialized America was obliterated. Mark Twain the business man was flattened; Mark Twain the author had to stand him up. Physically spent and morally disheartened, at the age of sixty he once again entered upon the activities he had repeatedly said he detested and wished never again to undertake, and traveled in order to lecture and to write another travel book. He did so, moreover, on a scale that dwarfed the journeys of his younger self, visiting almost every country in which an English-speaking audience could be expected to welcome him. Thanks to the British Empire, this meant a journey around the world.

Accompanied by his wife and their daughter Clara, Twain left Elmira, New York, in July 1895, lectured across the Midwest and West to Vancouver, sailed from there in late August, and read from his work and lectured some one hundred times in Australia, New Zealand, Ceylon, India, and South Africa. His public appearances stretched from Cleveland to Cape Town. In July 1896, a year after he had set out, his tour ended in England and there he settled to write *Following the Equator*, which was published in the following year. Although the profits from tour and book did erase his bankruptcy—he proudly repaid one hundred cents on the dollar and was returned to a financial comfort he enjoyed for the rest of his life—he told Howells, "I wrote my last travel book in hell; but I let on, the best I could, that it was an excursion through

Following the equator aboard the SS *Warrimoo*.
The John Work Garrett Library of The Johns Hopkins University

heaven. . . . How I did loathe that journey round the world!—
except the sea-part & India."[10]

The least-read today of Twain's travel books and in tone the
least cheerful of them, *Following the Equator* is, nevertheless, an
exceptional book, distinguished by a greater degree of authorial

self-awareness than had formerly been present in his travel accounts. Battered by a personal financial collapse that he could not but view also as a revelation of the flaws in the American economic system of boom and bust, he opened himself to the possibility that other ways of living the everyday life might be better than the American life of acquisitive hustle. In this his last travel book he finally departed from the stance of a defensive tourist alternately amused at the antic ways of foreigners and scornful of their un-American behavior, and he opened himself to what could be learned from them—especially to what it means to perceive that one's own culture is no more natural than that of others, and so to discard lifelong prejudices. The power of superior travel writing resides in the author's capacity to present his heightened self-awareness in a manner that moves readers to question the unexamined familiarities of their own lives. *Following the Equator* possesses this power.

Twain's journey led him through the colonized lands of color of the British Empire, and his anger at what he saw animates his pages. For example, of the Australian system whereby labor for the plantations is supplied by recruiters who transport boys from South Sea islands, he writes, "But for the meddling philanthropists, the native fathers and mothers would be fond of seeing their children carted into exile and now and then the grave, instead of weeping about it and trying to kill the kind recruiters." Ostensibly writing about the dingo, the wild dog of Australia, he says, "He has been sentenced to extermination, and the sentence will be carried out. This is all right and not objectionable. The world was made for man—the white man." Twenty-five years ago in *Roughing It* Twain had treated American Indians with contempt; they were scarcely human. Now, touring a museum in Australia, he is struck by the absence of any aboriginal artifacts and with his customary attention to linguistic precision grimly amused at the fact that the word "native" is applied only to Australian-born whites, the true natives being denoted by the classification "blackfellows." The home lesson about the mental annihilation of a native population is not lost on him. Abroad he carps at the true natives being unrepresented in the museum, but in America, he now realizes, the same is true. "It never struck me before," he admits. The outrage the treatment of the aboriginal population of Australia invoked was increased tenfold in Africa, where he wrote of the way whole populations in Rhodesia linger out a twenty-year death "with its daily burden of insult, humiliation, and forced labor for a man whose entire race the victim hates."

In pointed opposition to his contempt for the way of the white settlers, throughout *Following the Equator* Twain is enthralled by people of color. Earlier in his career when he had encountered the differences, the otherness of European and Near Eastern cultures, his customary response had been to see their divergence as a sign of their inferiority, at times even of a willed stupidity, as they lagged behind the technological advances of the nineteenth century. But as he wearily circled the globe after the collapse of his business enterprises, the exotic cultures he met spoke to him of other and possibly better ways of conducting one's daily life.

Instead of the gleeful narrator who had made joke after joke about Mormon polygamy in *Roughing It* or scorned what he called Italian "priestcraft" in *Innocents Abroad*, the Twain of *Following the Equator* is keenly interested in understanding the kinds of alien behavior he had once seized upon to raise a laugh. For example, he observes a Parsee funeral with its termination in the placement of the corpse on a "tower of silence," there to be wasted by the elements and consumed by carrion birds, and explains the way in which every aspect of the funeral is connected to a principle of purity. When on the hot plains outside Allahabad he comes upon roads crowded with pilgrims "who had come from all over India . . . plodding patiently along in the heat and dust, worn, poor, hungry, but sustained by an unwavering faith and belief," he notes that they are supremely happy because upon reaching the Ganges they will be cleansed from every vestige of sin. The notion that thenceforth whatever thing they touch, even the dead and rotten, will be made pure is not treated as explodable superstition but as awe-inspiring belief. The power of such faith is wonderful: "It is done in love, or it is done in fear; I do not know which it is. No matter what the impulse is, the act born of it is beyond imagination marvelous to our kind of people, the cold whites."

"The cold whites"—in Ceylon and again in India Twain is forcibly attracted to color: the color of skin, the color of garments, and the warm vitality they signify. The walking groups of Ceylonese clad in blues and purples, yellows and ruby reds make him catch his breath with joy as they sweep by him: "I looked at my women-folk's clothes," he says, "to recognize them as the dreary Sunday clothes of England and America, and was ashamed to be seen in the street with them. Then I looked at my own clothes and was ashamed to be seen in the street with myself." As is characteristically the case, when Twain fixes on the details of appearance, more than physical description is involved. The clothes of Americans in their drab propriety suppress the human instinct for color, grace, and harmony: "Yes, our clothes are a lie, and have been nothing short of that these hundred years. They are insincere, they are the ugly and appropriate outward exposure of an inward sham and moral decay."

Skin color also signifies more than meets the eye immediately: "Nearly all black and brown skins are beautiful, but beautiful white skin is rare. . . . Where dark complexions are massed, they make whites look bleached out, unwholesome, and sometimes frankly ghastly. I could notice them as a boy down South in the slavery days before the war." As this passage suggests, at the heart of Twain's remarkable surrender to color is the mechanism of his extraordinary memory and the manner in which it could erase time and instantly invoke a past experience when prompted by an incident in the present. And the past, to which he was returned time and again by the brown bodies in the lands he visited, was his boyhood in the days of slavery.

When the German proprietor of Twain's Bombay hotel showed him to his room, a native was there working on his knees to adjust the glazed door that opened onto the balcony. The proprietor walked over to the workman and, before stating what he wanted done, gave him a brisk cuff on the face. "I had not seen the like of this for fifty years. It carried me back to my boyhood, and flashed upon me the forgotten fact that this was the *usual* way of explaining one's desire to a slave."

Thus transported to the past, Twain remembered his father, a kindly man who nevertheless treated Lewis, "our harmless slave boy," in such a fashion, and then relives the moment when at the age of ten he witnessed a man fling a lump of iron ore at a slave in anger, killing him:

Nobody in the village approved of that murder; but of course no one said much about it. It is curious—the space annihilating power of thought. For just one second all that goes to make the *me* in me was in a Missourian village, on the other side of the globe, vividly seeing again those forgotten pictures of fifty years ago, and wholly unconscious of all things but just those; and in the next second I was back in Bombay, and the kneeling native's smitten cheek was not done tingling yet.

The injustices of the prewar South were so constantly present to Twain as he traveled that he registered the values of the peoples whose lands he visited with a sympathy, indeed an advocacy, that was new to his travel writing. His pages dealing with the dignity of native peoples and the despicable mendacity of their colonial exploiters foreshadow the social critic who was to become increasingly vehement in his attacks on imperialism. Awakened by his travel around the world, there emerged from beneath the surface of Twain's consciousness a mixture of loving memories of the gait, the voices, and the physical aura of slaves he had known, and gnawing memories of the everyday exercise of inhumanity toward them to which he had been a youthful, uncomplaining, and so consenting, witness. His fusion of adult experiences abroad with the memories they invoked of a youth spent among slaves is, in its understated eloquence, unmatched by his other writings on racial injustice.

In the nearly thirty years since he was an innocent abroad, the tourist who had responded to his differences from other peoples with a scorn for their inadequacies had developed into an advocate for the kinship of all peoples and an eloquent opponent of the imperialism upon which the United States embarked when it declared war upon Spain in 1898. Such advocacy, however, could not be advanced through laughter. Sarcasm overcame satire as in his final years the world's greatest humorist became its nagging conscience. He entered the public prints time and again to expose the lies offered in justification for the suppression of Philippine independence after Spain had been evicted from the archipelago. He did not hesitate to attack the glorification of war heroes who had supervised the well-armed American slaughter of Philippine insurgents who wanted what they had been promised when they fought with the Americans against Spain, and he faced down the accusations of antipatriotism that his stand evoked. "If there was any valuable difference between being an American and a monarchist," he said, "it lay in the theory that the American could decide for himself what is patriotic and what isn't; whereas the king could dictate the monarchist's patriotism for him."[11] William McKinley was not his king; neither was Theodore Roosevelt.

Sensitive to the worldwide affection for Twain, newspaper criticism of his anti-imperialism tended to steer away from his person and treat his opposition to American policy as that of a great humorist's misguidedly straying into serious matters upon which he was ill qualified to comment. But Twain would have none of it. As earlier in his career he had been irked at being seen as a mere funny man, so now he insisted that he would rather be attacked as a traitor than dismissed as a humorist.[12] When his good friend, the minister Joseph Twichell, cautioned him not to fly so in the face of public opinion—after all, he had only recently recovered from bankruptcy and it was senseless to jeopardize the sales upon which he could now rely—he replied: "You are a public guide and teacher, Joe, and are under a heavy responsibility to men, young and old; if you teach your people—as you teach me—to hide their opinions when they believe the flag is being abused and dishonored, lest the utterance do them and a publisher a damage, how do you answer for it to your conscience?"[13]

Harper's, his publisher, had exclusive rights to everything he wrote and would not allow him to publish some of the more vehement of his satires on American policy, or on the atrocities committed by colonial powers elsewhere in the world, as he extended his anti-imperialism to Africa and his antimonarchism to support for Russian revolutionaries. He did, however, manage to procure permission for the Congo Reform Association to issue "King Leopold's Soliloquy: A Defence of his Congo Rule," in twenty-five-cent booklet form, all proceeds to go to its cause. It is perhaps the bitterest of his acrimonious attacks on imperialism as his unbridled rage at the atrocities he recorded— what today is termed genocide—led to an unrelenting but rhetorically clumsy satire. In other pieces he more deftly discomfited the Christian missionaries who had exacted outrageous compensations from the Chinese for damage to life and property in the Boxer Rebellion. Since his days as a San Francisco journalist he had been an admirer of the self-sufficiency of the Chinese population in California and their poise under persecution, and his global tour had intensified his scorn for the uninvited impositions Christian missionaries visited upon native peoples in their homelands. He relished each missionary counterattack upon him in the public prints as occasion for another zestful sally against them.

As the travels that led to *Life on the Mississippi* had consequences beyond that book, most tellingly in the wonderfully realized settings and deepened themes of *Huckleberry Finn*, so those that led to *Following the Equator* had consequences beyond that book in anti-imperialist essays and tracts. Come what might, from the depths of his own humanity Mark Twain spoke out against the colonial powers and their self-righteous agents, the Christian missionaries. Even when his arguments turned into exasperated tirades, millions who read him could sense that the depths of fellow feeling that fed this outrage were identical with those that had fed his humor. He was still their Mark Twain—unshakably so.

Three

NOVELIST

ALTHOUGH MARK TWAIN'S LITERARY ACTIVITIES EXTENDED FOR SOME sixty years, from his newspaper apprenticeship in 1851 to his death in 1910, all seven of his full-length novels appeared in a twenty-one year period within that long span. His first novel, *The Gilded Age* (1873), written in collaboration with Charles Dudley Warner, was set in the time in which it was written, an era that has ever since borne the label given it in the book's title. Almost twenty years later he returned to the same setting and to some of the same characters in *The American Claimant* (1892), another political satire, while three other novels—*The Adventures of Tom Sawyer* (1876), *The Adventures of Huckleberry Finn* (1884), and *Pudd'nhead Wilson* (1894)—were set in the antebellum South of his boyhood, and two were set in an England of the imagined past—historical in *The Prince and the Pauper* (1882) and legendary in *A Connecticut Yankee in King Arthur's Court* (1889). Twain, however, never followed a novel within one of these groups with another from the same group, but over the years of his novel writing he interleaved them. As a consequence, although the settings place the novels in three distinct groups, their themes connect them in different patterns so that, for example, a boyish craving for high adventure and popular admiration in *Tom Sawyer* is echoed in the novel that followed, *The Prince and the Pauper*; the narrow-minded mores of village society in *Huckleberry Finn* are echoed in the behavior of peasant society in *Connecticut Yankee*. Twain was an avid reader of history. He delighted in visualizing the pageantry of the past and mimicking what he imagined to be the diction of an earlier day. But present in Arthurian or Tudor England, albeit in armor or tights, were the same men and boys and the same flawed patterns of social conduct that characterized the life led in nineteenth-century villages on the banks of the Mississippi.

Irritated by a piece of legislation having to do with the mails, Mark Twain responded by writing a paper on the issue. It began: "Reader, suppose you were an idiot. And suppose you were a member of Congress. But I repeat myself." He never published it. Writing had served to relieve his exasperation, and publications that were apt to excite opposition and so require him to devote a good amount of time to rebuttals had to be reserved for larger game. "Sometimes my feelings are so hot," he wrote, "I have to take the pen and put them on paper to keep them from setting me afire inside; then all that ink and labor are wasted because I can't print the result."[1] Still, the "waste" was not waste but an exercise that conserved the time and restored the equanimity essential for his authorship.

No American novelist before Twain had been so concerned as was he with the daily world of American politics. He had strong opinions on just about every current event that came to his attention from trivial postal regulations to buccaneering congressional raids on public funds, and the nation frequently heard from him on these matters. "Whether or not his opinions on politics and economics are convincing now," Louis J. Budd wrote in his valuable summary of Twain's social philosophy, "they were in the final analysis sincerely held and backed by more cold reasons than those of the average modern intellectual who turns his back on public affairs."[2] If Twain often pleased the public with what might be termed "safe ridicule"—funny as the remark is, nothing is at risk when he says, for example, that there is no distinctly native American criminal class except Congress—he was also willing to hazard public favor by refusing to let pass political practices that he regarded as stupid or corrupt, regardless of the power of those who endorsed them or the popularity they enjoyed.

His professional writing career had commenced with his duties as a political reporter covering the doings of the Nevada legislature, and his subsequent journalism from California, Hawaii, New York, and, for a very brief spell in 1867 from Washington, had always been in some part concerned with the politics of the locale from which he reported, although he tended increasingly to concentrate on feature stories rather than political reports. Even in his advanced years with his newspaper days far behind him, Twain retained his reportorial instincts; in 1898, for example, while residing in Vienna after the completion of *Following the Equator*, he sent back to America lengthy dispatches on the tumultuous political scene in that capital.

It is not remarkable, then, that Twain's career as a novelist began with *The Gilded Age*, a satire on the widespread political corruption of his day that featured fictionalized portraits of recognizable politicians and their illegal activities, nor that his collaborator, Charles Dudley Warner, editor of the *Hartford Courant*, was a reforming journalist. More notable is the fact that although after this initial novelistic venture he continued to attack the specific social and political iniquities and stupidities of his day in essays and letters, in his novels he turned his concern from particular instances of breakdown within the social system to a consideration of the system itself. In both the historical romances and the Mississippi novels the theme of the inescapable vulnerabilities of democratic polity is dramatized in the contrast between the benevolent motives of clear-eyed characters such as Huck Finn, Pudd'nhead Wilson, Miles Hendon (of *The Prince and the Pauper*), or Hank Morgan (the Connecticut Yankee), and the fear, superstition, and avarice that govern community behavior, be it in Arkansas or in Camelot.

The division of the collaborators' labor in *The Gilded Age* is apparent. Twain's plot is that of political shenanigans, and Warner's that of love long deferred and finally realized. But, just as clearly, each author's knowledge assisted the other's plot: Twain's mining experience figures in the profession of Warner's clean-cut young hero, the only character in the novel who seeks his fortune by working hard and working honestly, and Warner's knowledge of political rascality enriches Twain's depiction of lobbyists and lawmakers.

The theme of the novel, if one can be said to emerge from this portrait of a world in which the best way to get rich quick is to procure legislation that will channel public funds into the enhancement of private property, is that sturdy individualism can win out over the forces of corporate enterprise and political corruption.[3] It is an argument that in actual experience became increasingly frayed with the seemingly unstoppable rise of the great trusts in the last decades of the century. Indeed, Twain himself emerged from bankruptcy at century's end thanks in great part to the volunteered financial management of his funds by Henry H. Rogers, a prince in the feudality of American monopolists noted for the ruthlessness of his business dealings. Still, since it was Rogers's management of the funds that belonged to Twain (rather than any money he gave to Twain) that assisted in the recovery, Twain could even then, a quarter-century after *The Gilded Age*, still believe that individual labor could reverse financial ruin.

The literary rewards of *The Gilded Age*, as opposed to its historical value as one of the defining documents of its era, reside in the character of Colonel Sellers.[4] An indefatigable optimist, Sellers goes to Washington to seek legislation to fund the dredging of the insignificant stream that trickles by his backwoods property, converting it into a navigable river that will bring to his land both commerce and the townships that already exist fully built in his imagination. In contrast to the tone of moral reprobation that attaches to other schemers in the novel, the Colonel retains an air of sublime innocence because the failures of his schemes only inspire him to successively more imaginative accounts of how the setbacks are really triumphs. His guileless ability to explain away the apparently incontrovertible facts that constantly spring up to contradict him is boundless, a triumph of spirit over the material world in an era of greed.

I have been reading up some European Scientific reports—friend of mine, Count Fugier, sent them to me—sends me all sorts of things from Paris—he thinks the world of me Fugier does. Well, I saw that the Academy of France had been testing the properties of heat, and they came to the conclusion that it was a non-conductor or something like that, and of course its influence must be deadly in nervous organizations with excitable temperaments, especially when there is any tendency toward rheumatic affections. Bless you I saw in a moment what was the matter with us, and says I, out goes your fires!—no more slow tortures and certain death for me, sir. What you want is the *appearance* of heat, not the heat itself—that's the idea.

This is the reason the glow on the isinglass window of the Colonel's stove is made by a candle's flame rather than a fire, and why those huddled around that stove are not *really* cold. The manifest lack of fuel is irrelevant. "Rheumatism? Why a man can't any more start a case of rheumatism in this house than he can shake an opinion out of a mummy!" And so the shivering guest no longer shivers but goes to his cold bed warmed by the Colonel's rhetoric.

Colonel Sellers is a theatrical figure. Whenever he appears the book lights up. His performances stand out from the novel's teeming subplots, and, perceiving this, an enterprising playwright produced a script that centered on Sellers's character rather than the web of incidents in the novel. Twain purchased the script, then in effect scrapped it and wrote his own stage version, a play that was *Colonel Sellers* rather than *The Gilded Age*. For a number of years the actor John T. Raymond toured in the role, making himself synonymous with it; more than $100,000 appears a conservative estimate of the profits that he and Twain shared.[5]

Twain had welcomed the opportunity to write the play; the novel on which he had set to work after *The Gilded Age* had slowed to a halt and lay dormant awaiting further inspiration. But some time in 1875, when Raymond brought the play to Hartford, Twain's inspiration revived and he brought *The Adventures of Tom Sawyer* to completion. Twain did not attend the Hartford performances, and in a letter read to the audience by Raymond explained why. He had always, he said, taken pride in making his money outside of Hartford, the city in which he lived, but now, "at this late day I find myself in the crushed and bleeding position of fattening myself upon the spoils of my brethren! Can I support such grief as this? (This is literary emotion, you understand. Take the money at the door just the same.)"[6] Whatever might have been the real reason that Twain chose to conceal by such joking, it is clear that in putting the play behind him he was freshened to return to the strongest sources of his creative imagination, his memories of the river and his boyhood. *Life on the Mississippi* and *Huckleberry Finn* were to follow *Tom Sawyer*. Mark Twain was in his prime.

The Adventures of Tom Sawyer takes its rise in Twain's memories of his boyhood in Hannibal, Missouri, in the 1840s. Although some of the incidents in the novel are based on actual experiences, the novel does not so much consist of his representation of specific events in which he took part as it does of his representation of the mentality of boyhood itself. In a world in which only adults are important Tom dreams of winning fame—and so the envy of his peers—and each of his adventures ingeniously attains that end for a glorious moment before the adult world closes in, and he must respond by devising another scheme. Tom is Colonel Sellers reversed, converting his imaginings into reality whereas the Colonel converted reality into an imagined condition.

Tom's adventures do not follow one another in any necessary order because Twain is not concerned with the evolution of Tom's character—with his movement from one stage of childhood to a later one—but, rather, with capturing examples of the unsuspicious response to the capacities of life that are characteristic of boyhood. E. L. Doctorow persuasively suggests that the alternation between fantasy and fulfillment that marks Tom's adventures resembles the process of authorship because, like an author, Tom is constantly engaged in bringing into being what he has imagined. "Possibly," Doctorow writes, "we are ourselves witness to the author's exploratory method of composition, in which he first conceives of likely things for a boy's mind to imagine, and then decides some of them are too good not to be developed and played out as elements of a plot. In any event a godlike power of realization is conferred upon Tom, as if authorship itself is transferred, and we see a causal connection in what he seriously and intensely imagines and what comes to pass."[7]

Boys in the actual world become men, but in Twain's remembered world boyhood is a space in which time hangs suspended. Decades before Tom, Charles Dickens's boys—Oliver Twist, Nicholas Nickleby, David Copperfield—had all appeared already darkened by the shadows of their approaching adulthood. But none of Tom's adventures alters his character or matures him— he is always the boy he was—and the village of St. Petersburg in which he lives correspondingly remains suspended in time, immune from the harrying of history. Even its villains—be they smarmy Sid or murderous Injun Joe—have an innocent glow as if they are only meeting their duty to be nasty. For a brief time after completing the novel, Twain wondered whether he had written a story for children or a book for adults. The answer, he really knew, was that he had done both. The children's adventures are fare for children, but the state of childhood itself is a domain that can be visited with effect only by those who have left it.

Twain had initially pondered telling Tom's story in the first person. His decision not to was sound. Tom is a bright boy who has fed his imagination with a good deal of romantic reading; to have narrated in his voice would have been to limit the novel's viewpoint to what is, finally, a conventional if lively sensibility, and so lose the special adult quality of nostalgic affection for a time of life that even with its occasional disappointments was, in retrospect, happier. Third-person narration permitted a greater descriptive range without qualifying the novel's sustained theme of boyhood as a condition rather than a time. If Tom had told the tale, his perpetual romancing would not have permitted the slyly funny sketches that, in their amused, if also affectionate, attitude toward the earnest simplicities of village life, keep nostalgia from becoming mawkish. Tom would not, for example, have been able to supply the sharply realized pictures of the prize recitations at the village school. There: "A very little boy stood up and recited, 'You'd scarce expect one of my age to speak in public on the stage, etc.' accompanying himself with the painfully exact and spasmodic gesture which a machine might have used—supposing the machine to be a trifle out of order." Another participant was "a slim melancholy girl whose face had the interesting paleness that comes of pills and indigestion." And another recitation that began: "'Dark and tempestuous was the night' . . . occupied some ten pages of manuscript and wound up with a sermon so destructive of all hope to non-Presbyterians that it took the first prize." The phrasing of these instant sketches, the way in which the final clause of each moves counter to, yet completes, what preceded it, is the work of an accomplished platform performer. We can sense the precisely timed pause before the quiet crash of the modifying phrase or clause that closes the description and triggers laughter. Such artistry enhances the essential good cheer of the novel as a whole and would have been unavailable in Tom's voice.

The river serves as splendid backdrop to the unchanging scenery of Tom Sawyer's world, as fixed as is the village that borders it. But the mighty Mississippi pushes unstoppably through *Huckleberry Finn*, bringing the passage of time with it. It is a pathway to freedom and a road to enslavement, the realm of an idyll beyond history and the unstemmable stream of history itself. The world of *Huckleberry Finn* is not the world of *Tom Sawyer*. After completing the earlier novel, Twain had revisited the river of his youth and, with his decision to let Huck tell his story, a more complex sensibility takes control and makes more complex demands upon his artistry.

> I felt so mournful I most wished I was dead. The stars was shining, and the leaves rustled in the woods ever so mournful; and I heard an owl away off, who-whooing about somebody that was dead, and a whippowill and a dog crying about somebody that was going to die; and the wind was trying to whisper something to me and I couldn't make out what it was, and so it made the cold shivers run over me.

These are the imaginings of Huck in the world of Huck. The dread he feels as the sounds of nature flow in on him is the primal fear of the dark and the inhuman that religions are designed to counter. But "uncivilized" Huck's imagination lingers in the instinctual world of superstition, and as the novel progresses—the quoted passage occurs in the early pages—the civilized world opposed to it is turned upside down. The most religious people in the novel, the plain and humble Phelpses and the members of their congregation, are those who act as slave catchers, while in their pursuit of freedom Huck and Jim are guided by a web of superstitions that, unlike religious doctrine, can interpret the coded messages of nature and alert them to the treachery of men.

The quoted passage consists of compound sentences: simple declarative statements joined together by "and" and "and" and "and." Whereas in complex sentences separate clauses are knit into a rationally apprehensible whole through the use of connectives such as "therefore," "but," and "whereas," which establish relationships of causality and dependency, the unity of effect that Twain achieves is poetic rather than rational. The emotional integrity of Huck's sensibility emerges from his rhythmic use of alliteration; thirteen words begin with "w," the most suggestive of them with "wh" as well; from half-rhymes whose muted echoes in series such as "mournful," "mournful," "owl," and "whippowill" bind the sentences aurally; and from the wavering pulse of repetitions—"dead," "dead," "die;" "somebody," "somebody" "something." In elevating American speech into expressiveness Twain did not copy its features literally—informal speech is fragmentary, often ungrammatical, and larded with hesitations and resumptions that repeat words before advancing—but simulated them to uncover the poetic infrastructure of the American vernacular. "All modern American literature comes from one book by Mark Twain called *Huckleberry Finn*," said Ernest Hemingway.

Deprived by Huck's viewpoint of the opportunity to make the same kind of jokes he did in *Tom Sawyer*, Twain relies upon Huck's ability to depict what he sees precisely in imagery that is both startlingly original, yet grounded in the homely actualities of his back country life. The undertaker whose aplomb he greatly admires was the "softest, glindingest stealthiest man I ever see; and there warn't no more smile to him than there is to a ham." The duke whose hypocritical imitation of a deaf mute all but sickens Huck, "went a goo-gooing around, happy and satisfied, like a jug that's googling out buttermilk."

Accepting the fact that there must be some good reason for social behavior that, in his ignorance, seems to him to be cruel, stupid, or groundless, Huck is soberly wary of the underside of whatever he encounters. Although he recognizes the evil in the plans of the Duke and Dauphin or in the murderous conduct of the men he overhears on the wrecked steamboat, and knows such villains to be far worse than the majority of the fallible persons he encounters along his journey, he still cannot accept the fact that they deserve to receive the unfeeling treatment they have inflicted upon others. Witnessing the tarred and feathered Duke and Dauphin, men who have consistently and viciously betrayed him, he says, "Well, it made me sick to see it; and I was sorry for them poor pitiful rascals, it seemed like I could never feel any hardness against them any more in the world. It was a dreadful thing to see. Human beings *can* be awful cruel to one another."

While in the river communities regulated by civil laws and religious strictures, right-and-wrong, good-and-bad are opposites, to Huck's instinctive perception such differences are matters of degree, not kind, and those who tar and feather in the performance of justice in effect reveal their kinship with those whom they punish.

Regardless of the motive for its exercise, cruelty is cruelty, and, Huck notes, it is a human possession. That every one of the large and varied range of characters he encounters in his journey would unhesitatingly return Jim to slavery serves as a constant reminder to him that his participation in a flight to freedom (his own as well as Jim's) is antisocial and therefore wrong, and as a constant reminder to the reader of the ambiguous status of "conscience": either the monitor of conduct in the service of religious and social strictures or the principle of conduct that transcends such strictures. In acting in response to the dictates of his conscience, Huck believes himself to be acting against conscience.

Increasingly in his writings after *Huckleberry Finn*, Twain was to insist upon the inherent selfishness of all humans—a circumstance akin to what his elders would have called human depravity. Yet he was a humorist, and *Huckleberry Finn*, even with its scenes of violence, fraud, and gullibility, is also a comic masterpiece, its humor flowing from a display of the immeasurable range of antics that can arise from the constitutional foolishness of mankind. The universality of human folly is but the comic corollary of the dire theological principle of inherent sin.

The Prince and the Pauper appeared between *Tom Sawyer* and *Huckleberry Finn*, and, although it falls well below their level of achievement, its setting in sixteenth-century England can, perhaps, be credited as providing Twain a space within which to draw his creative breath between the major achievements of the Mississippi boyhood books. Despite their outrage at critics who scoffed at humorous writing as second-rate literature, his family and friends felt that he was yet to make the contribution to the national literature of which he was capable. *The Prince and the Pauper* was intended to show what he could do in a more serious vein. Twain was a shrewd interpreter of literary trends, whatever the shortcomings of his foresightedness in matters of financial investment. As it turned out, historical romance was to become a very popular genre in the decade that followed *The Prince and the Pauper*, with such best-selling examples as *When Knighthood Was in Flower* by Charles Major and *Alice of Old Vincennes* by Maurice Thompson. But although popular, *The Prince and the Pauper* was not a critical success. An English reviewer wrote, "If to convert a brilliant and engaging humorist into a dull and painful romancer be necessarily the function of the study of history, it cannot be too steadily discouraged."[8]

Through an improbable accident, which nevertheless quite acceptably sets the novel in motion, Tom Canty, child of the London slums, changes places with Prince Edward—the Edward VI to be. While Tom the pauper manages, fumblingly at first, to exercise his royal powers to alleviate the harshness of laws founded on the inherited right of the few to rule pitilessly over the many, the prince is launched onto the streets of London and then upon the roads of England to witness the suffering of his people under unjust laws. Tom Canty's streetwise behavior and his flight from a brutal father relate him to Huck Finn, while Prince Edward's flair for adventure and unflagging confidence in his superiority, even when all circumstances are opposed, relate him to Tom Sawyer.

As a story essentially for children, *The Prince and the Pauper* has its charm. Critics from Twain's day to this have been too hard on it. The enjoyment Twain conveys in dramatizing the results of his research into the court and street life of Tudor England is infectious, and in an attractively managed foreshadowing of Jim's relation to Huck, Miles Hendon, Edward's adult companion on his outcast travels, although vastly his inferior by law, serves morally to mature him. Once they are on the road the novel gains in vivacity, Twain's imagination characteristically expanding when travel invites a subordination of plot as a whole to the separate stories encountered along the route.

When he entered sixteenth-century England, however, Twain did not take with him his unique power to guarantee the reality of his fictive world through a vernacular style that tied it to his reader's world. In order for prince and pauper to be mistaken for one another they had, with few differences, to speak in the same fashion, which is to say, bookishly. Worse, the third-person narrator himself falls into the bogus diction he has confected for his characters. When he speaks of boys "disporting themselves, and right noisily too," the "right" jars badly as a deviation from, almost an insult to, the standard of diction Twain characteristically demanded from himself as well as others. People who talk like this in Twain's other writings unconsciously reveal a falseness that may sometimes be hidden even from themselves but cannot hide from their speech. The Duke and the Dauphin might talk like that, not Mark Twain. For the space of a novel in which he reached for acceptance as a serious writer, however, Mark Twain did. And when the "swarm" who live in Offal Court are called "human vermin," who gives them that label? Not the prince and not the pauper, but the narrator who permits his detestation of injustice to lead him to a contempt for its victims, a disposition that cuts against the theme of the iniquity of a social order based on the inherited power of the few and the inescapable powerlessness of the many. It is as if for a moment the narrator shares the nobility's contempt for the people at large.

But although the setting of *A Connecticut Yankee in King Arthur's Court* is again an England of sharp class distinction and consequent injustices, *Huckleberry Finn* has come between it and *The Prince and the Pauper*, and Twain entered upon it with a full realization of the expressive range he could achieve through vernacular speech. Hank Morgan, the Connecticut Yankee, tells the tale.

In Edward Bellamy's *Looking Backward, 2000–1887,* which had appeared in 1888, the year before *Connecticut Yankee,* Julian West, a Bostonian, falls asleep to awaken in 2000, a time in which the dreadful human cost of the private control of industry, which had dismayed him in 1887, has been replaced by a social and economic collectivism that has eradicated poverty, crime, and war. Ignatius Donnelly's *Caesar's Column,* published in the following year, that in which *A Connecticut Yankee* also appeared, originated in the same social concerns that motivated Bellamy but took an apocalyptic view of the future that awaited America. In it an aristocracy of plutocrats, which ruthlessly ruled the country, is opposed by a revolutionary movement that overthrows it—only to perish in the debacle of greed and lust that follows upon the sudden emancipation of the great mass of economic slaves. Then five years after *A Connecticut Yankee,* William Dean Howells offered his version of the socialist utopia of the future in *A Traveler from Altruria.* Twain's novel was, thus, surrounded by two utopias and a dystopia, all agreeing that, in its late century manifestation, American capitalism tended toward the destruction of democratic order and maimed the lives of tens of thousands of workers, morally as well as physically.

Like those futuristic novels of social criticism, *A Connecticut Yankee* also addresses the human consequences of an economy driven by the forces of centralizing industrialization but does so from the other end, as it were: looking at the condition of humanity *before* those economic forces existed. Hank Morgan travels to a past in which the mass of humankind is kept in abject subjection to an oligarchy made up of loutish knights and in perpetual fear by a clergy that strictly enforces popular ignorance. With modern Yankee know-how he sets about liberating the nation from these restraints. The utopia toward which Hank moves is nineteenth-century America with its factories, schools, newspapers, representative government, electric lights, telephones, telegraphs, and other mechanical enhancements of everyday life. Yet with that utopia having been effectively achieved over the course of the novel, Hank's narrative ends with its apocalyptic ruin and a return to a darkness even deeper than that which preceded his arrival. *A Connecticut Yankee*, that is, constructs a utopia only to see it implode despite Hank's—and, one suspects, Twain's—best efforts.

When Hank Morgan, a foreman of the Colt arms factory in Hartford, awakes in King Arthur's England he is, at first, uncertain as to just where he is as he gazes upon all the strangely dressed and oddly speaking people. But, with characteristic Yankee practicality, uncertainty incites rather than deters decision:

> I made up my mind to two things; if it was still the nineteenth century and I was among lunatics and couldn't get away, I would presently boss that asylum or know the reason why; and if on the other hand it was really the sixth century, all right, I didn't want any softer thing: I would boss the whole country inside of ten months; for I judge I would have the start of the best-educated man in the kingdom by a matter of thirteen hundred years and upwards.

His attitude is both invigorating and familiar: Tom Sawyer as adult, still confident of his ability to bring into being what he imagines but now relying on a knowledge of mechanics rather than books of adventure to serve as his resource.

After he becomes "Sir Boss," Hank's first act is to establish a patent office, "for I knew that a country without a patent office and good patent laws was just a crab, and couldn't travel any way but sideways or backwards"; next, a school system and a newspaper. He overcomes the resistance of the entrenched oligarchy of knights and clergy by introducing private enterprise and civil liberties, but conceals the mechanical means he employs to produce his major effects, permitting the people to believe that he possesses supernatural powers. "It occurred to me," Hank writes, "that these animals didn't reason; that *they* never put this and that together." Given a nation of such "animals," one did not lead by rational means: "Unlimited power *is* the thing when it is in safe hands," he says.

Hank's calling the people "animals" echoes the narrator's labeling of the slum dwellers in *The Prince and the Pauper* as "vermin." At best this attitude can be accepted as the irruption of an understandable exasperation at the human reluctance to shed prejudices in the light of reason. Yet since this attitude justifies unlimited power, it subterraneously pulls against Hank's expressed belief that training is everything, which is to say dystopia is ever present beneath the surface of utopia.

Hank defeats all challenging knights in a tournament by killing them with a revolver before they can reach him with their lances, then announces: "Knight-errantry was a doomed institution. The march of civilizations was begun." He is aware of the paradox of merging killing with the advancement of civilization and reconciles it through analogy with the French Revolution:

There were two "Reigns of Terror," if we would but remember it and consider it . . . the one lasted mere months, the other had lasted a thousand years; the one inflicted death upon ten thousand persons, the other upon a hundred millions, but our shudders are all for the 'horrors' of the minor Terror, the momentary Terror, so to speak, whereas, what is the horror of swift death by the axe compared with life-long death from hunger, cold, insult, cruelty and heart break? . . . that unspeakably bitter and awful Terror which none of us has been taught to see in its vastness or pity as it deserves.

With such a passage, Hank's being a Yankee takes on an added dimension: he is not just a Yankee in the sense of a shrewd, practical, jack-of-all-trades; he is also a Yankee in the sense of being an adherent to Tom Paine's revolutionary exercise of reason that dispassionately destroys all that is deemed irrational.

"A man *is* a man at bottom," Hank insists. "Whole ages of abuse and oppression cannot crush the manhood out of him." Still, despite such affirmations, the undertow of prejudicial attachment to inherited traditions—however irrational—eventually pulls Arthur's England back from its nineteenth-century utopia into its original, uncluttered condition, mentally dark yet lit by a pastoral sun undimmed by factory smoke. At novel's conclusion, Hank's technical achievements are reduced to the dynamite with which he blows up his industries so that they will not fall into the hands of the resurgent oligarchy, and the electric fence that stands between the fifty-four allies remaining to him and an entire population that has gone back to the beliefs that have enslaved them. "English knights can be killed, but they cannot be conquered," Hank says; at the end the electrocuted bodies of twenty-five thousand men decomposing around his besieged camp prevent any escape except that of his awakening in Hartford. Yet he awakens with a longing for his sixth-century wife with her simple-minded, unreasoning reliance upon tradition, and with nostalgia for the unthinking nobility of character represented by King Arthur.

Even in this, the most expansive fictional presentation of his social philosophy, Twain often yields to his tendency to pursue the comic possibilities of a situation regardless of possible damage to his theme. Knights ride to the rescue on bicycles and patrol the land as sandwich men advertising soap, the broken-letter typography of a backwoods newspaper with its disjointed, slangy prose is mimicked in Camelot's first newspaper, and the Round Table is converted into a stock exchange. Of such shenanigans Bernard De Voto wrote, "The satirist's intention is constantly frustrated by the frontier humorist. The mere joke maker, the parodist, the creator of burlesque and extravaganza, the improvisator horribly mangles what might have been a superb book."[9] Quite so, although if less than superb, the book remains remarkably engrossing.

A Connecticut Yankee was written just before Mark Twain's descent into bankruptcy. Whether at the time of composition he was already painfully aware that his world would soon slide into disarray, it is difficult to say. One is tempted to read the murderous destruction of the nineteenth-century utopia Hank constructs as at least a semiconscious realization on Twain's part that something was deeply wrong with his own nineteenth-century world. Yet, on the other hand, the novel also affirms a belief that daily life in his time is better than it had been at any time in human history.

In the first half of the nineteenth century, writers such as Emerson, Hawthorne, and Melville, shaped by a more rural economy, remained apart from activities that their writings criticized as socially destructive and personally demeaning. But Twain plunged into the industrial economy of his day, an adventurer in the marketplace of capitalism pursuing goals that his fictions satirized as at best illusory and at worst destructive. After him, Theodore Dreiser and F. Scott Fitzgerald, to name but two, also conducted their lives in response to the very attractions that their fictions exposed as meretricious. With *A Connecticut Yankee*, a novel at war with itself yet absorbing in every detail, Mark Twain foreshadowed the ambiguous condition of the modern American writer, exposing the false values of his acquisitive society in his writings while pursuing its financial and social rewards in his personal life.

In 1892 the Clemenses shut their Hartford house and left for Europe, there to live more economically (although far from uncomfortably) in an effort to fend off bankruptcy. The family-owned publishing house was in the doldrums, and close to $200,000 had disappeared into the perpetually faulty Paige typesetter. Money that had supported these enterprises had come from Mark Twain's writings, and further writing now appeared as the only possible source of income in the immediate future. Twain's search for a profitable project led him back to Colonel Sellers—he was also later to attempt revivals of Tom and Huck—and in 1892 the Colonel reappeared in *The American Claimant*, the weakest of his novels.

The American claimant of the title is Colonel Sellers but, unlike his presence in *The Gilded Age*, here there is no plot without him. In the earlier novel, the delight he afforded was generated by the ingenuity with which his tireless imagination countered the realities that opposed it. But elevated above the plot in the later novel, the Colonel is, unfortunately, permitted to disregard rather than counter physical reality; and his schemes—to control sunspots or to materialize the dead—soar away from a necessary baseline of reality and in their sheer impossibility are both ridiculous and, as they go on and on, tedious.

Yet, faulty as it is, *The American Claimant* possesses a strong interest because of the refracted view it provides of the troubled mind of Mark Twain at that stage of his life. He was hurting from more than impending financial ruin when he wrote the novel. Matthew Arnold's criticism (published in 1888) still stung; in the novel Twain attempted to answer it both directly, by intruding into it a long speech in which an American newspaper editor attacks Arnold's book, and implicitly, in the story of the romance between Sellers's daughter and an English Viscount who travels incognito in order to test the values of American democracy and ends up admiring them. "What a civilization it is," Tracy (the disguised Viscount Berkeley) enthuses, "and what prodigious results these are! and brought about almost wholly by common men; not by Oxford-trained aristocrats, but men who stand shoulder-to-shoulder in the humble ranks of life and earn the bread that they eat."

There had always been a strain of anti-intellectualism in the travel books written before this novel. In his eagerness to bypass the conventions of travel writing, Twain had sometimes chosen to confirm the plain folk in their distrust of high culture as an affectation of the socially elite opposed to their democratic values, rather than to suggest that one of the results of democracy was that aesthetic pleasures were no longer restricted to that class but were available to all who sought access to them. His anti-intellectualism had, however, been qualified by his admitted uncertainty about his own cultural maturity. If, for example, he derided the Old Masters, in doing so he was also consciously exposing the degree of his own ignorance and leaving uncurtained the window through which more light might flow. In *The American Claimant*, however, high culture was embodied in a specific enemy, Matthew Arnold, and in the heat of his resentment Twain confounded the cultivated critic with cultivation itself and scorned the value of an educated intelligence. He clung to the essentially vulgar social outlook of the go-getting economy that had gone wrong for him, not yet aware that the valid refutation of Arnold's dismissal of the "funny man" did not reside in scorning high-mindedness but was already present in the brilliant critical analyses of human nature and human society to be found in *Huckleberry Finn* and other "funny" writings by Mark Twain.

When the very people to whom Hank Morgan strives to bring the political rights and material benefits of nineteenth-century civilization ally themselves with the forces that would keep them in their abject condition, he reflects, "It reminded me of a time thirteen centuries away, when the 'poor whites' of our South who were always despised and frequently insulted by the slave-lords around them, and who owed their base condition to the presence of slavery, did also finally shoulder their muskets and pour out their lives in an effort to prevent the destruction of that very institution which degraded them." Another incident reminds Hank of the 'infernal law" that had existed in the South in his time under which "freemen who could not prove that they were freemen had been sold into life-long slavery." Two years later in *The Tragedy of Pudd'nhead Wilson* (1894), the last of his novels, Mark Twain returned again to the small-town society of his boyhood, beginning his story in the 1830s and centering it on the institution of slavery and its crippling consequences. But unlike its presence in *Huckleberry Finn*, the institution as it is treated in *Pudd'nhead* is viewed through the lens of the collapse of the Reconstruction that followed emancipation. *Pudd'nhead Wilson* is concerned not just with slavery but with race and the twinned identities of black man and white man.

The theme of twinning that sinews the plot of *Pudd'nhead Wilson* had run through a number of Twain's previous works. In the coincidental sense of two unrelated persons with identical features, it forms the basis of *The Prince and the Pauper*. In the psychological sense of two different persons who together form a whole Huck and Tom may be seen as twinned. In shorter pieces Twain played with the comic possibilities of biological twins; and although his pen name signified to him a depth safe for navigation, he was well aware of its also connoting a splitting.

"An Encounter with an Interviewer," published in 1875, is in the form of a dialogue between a dapper young reporter and the narrator who personifies one of Twain's most effective comic personas, the "inspired idiot" who is apparently oblivious to the incongruities and consequent absurdity of what he says. At one point the interviewer asks his subject whether he has any brothers or sisters, and he replies that he thinks so but doesn't remember. Like other of Twain's "knowing" characters—for example, the narrator of the jumping frog story—the interviewer lacks a sense of humor, and exasperated by the incongruities through which he has been soberly navigating points to a picture on the wall: "Isn't that a brother of yours?" Yes, he is answered, it is brother Bill but there is an uncertainty as to whether he is dead although he has been buried.

Q. *Buried* him! *Buried* him without knowing whether he was dead or not?

A. O, no! Not that. He was dead enough.

Q. Well, I confess that I can't understand this. If you buried him and you knew he was dead.

A. No! no! We only thought he was.

Q. O, I see! He came to life again?

A. I bet he didn't.

Q. Well, I never heard anything like this. *Somebody* was dead. *Somebody* buried. Now, where was the mystery?

A. Ah, that's just it! That's it exactly. You see, we were twins,— defunct and I,— and we got mixed in the bath-tub when we were only two weeks old, and one of us was drowned. But we didn't know which. Some think it was Bill. Some think it was me.

Q. Well, that is remarkable. What do *you* think?

A. Goodness knows! I would give whole worlds to know.

Sam Clemens, to be sure, had no twin, but the relationship between Clemens and Twain is yet another form of twinning—with one submerged and the other present. Moreover, even freed of the presence of Clemens, Twain himself is double, a consummate satirist yet an author insistent upon making his mark by writing "seriously." After *Pudd'nhead* he published *Personal Recollections of Joan of Arc* (1896), a book on which he claimed he had been working for fourteen years, twelve in research and two in composition. Although it is classified as nonfiction it reads like historical romance. Twain regarded it as a companion piece to *The Prince and the Pauper,* which is to say as a work of major literary importance. Initially he had hoped to publish it anonymously so as to free it of a readership that would anticipate humor if his name were attached to it. Although this did not occur, it was the first of his books to be published under a new arrangement that gave Harper & Brothers exclusive rights to his work and so finally signified his departure from the subscription market and entry into the bookstores—and thus into a traditional form of literary respectability. Instead of pointing the reader toward additional books touted by canvassers, the endpapers of *Joan* advertised other Harper publications under the genteel heading, "Some Books for the Library." To the end of his life Twain believed *Joan* to be the best of his works, the supreme example of his mastery of the literary art, and in his enthusiasm convinced his family and even the rarely uncritical Paine that this was so.

More than one hundred years later, *Joan*, an effusive rhapsody, seems one of the worst of Twain's books. Over its entire 460 pages its tone is one of ceaseless praise, indeed, adoration, with the conclusion again saying what had been said countless times in the earlier pages: "I have finished my story of Joan of Arc, that wonderful child, that sublime personality, that spirit which in one regard has had no peer and will have none—this: purity from all alloy of self-seeking interest, personal ambition." And more distressing even than such unrelenting idolizing is the deafness that closes down upon Twain's marvelous ear for the spoken language. A peasant speaks: "Would you leave doing these wonders that make you be praised by everybody while there is still so much glory to be won?" A nobleman speaks: "They could not unglue their minds from these grandeurs and were wrenching the conversation out of its grooves." The drowned "literary" twin had resurfaced while the vernacular satirist sank from sight.

But *Pudd'nhead Wilson* reveals that satirist at his most biting and the theme of twinning at its most telling. Twain had long toyed with the jokes that could be teased from the situation of Siamese twins with totally different dispositions so that, for example, the teetotaling twin becomes drunk against his principles when his brother imbibes. The situation can be reversed, and the pious twin can drag his irreligious brother to sit through a tedious church service and be switched back again to involve the proper twin in misbehavior. But it is essentially the same joke; while Twain could not do much more with it, he, nevertheless, could not let it go. So in 1830 such twins (arriving from Italy, of all places) turn up in Dawson's Landing on the Missouri side of the Mississippi, and although it has since been abbreviated to *Pudd'nhead Wilson*, the full title of the novel published in 1894 is *The Tragedy of Pudd'nhead Wilson and the Comedy of Those Extraordinary Twins*. Recognizing their limitations, however, Twain soon moved the Italian twins to the margin of his plot even though he could not bring himself to abandon them entirely. *Pudd'nhead Wilson* centers on another set of twins, a pair who personify the unerasable bond of kindred between the black and white races in the United States even as their society insists upon maintaining an unbridgeable distance between them.

On February 1, 1830, two boys are born in the household of Percy Northumberland Driscoll, one to his wife and the other to Roxy his slave. Driscoll's wife dies within a week of giving birth, and Roxy is put in charge of both children:

To all intents and purposes Roxy was as white as anybody, but the one-sixteenth of her which was black out-voted the other fifteen parts and made her a negro. She was a slave and salable as such. Her child was thirty-one parts white, and he, too, was a slave and by a fiction of law and custom a negro. He had blue eyes and flaxen curls like his white comrade, but even the father of the white child was able to tell the children apart—little as he had commerce with them—by their clothes; for the white babe wore ruffled soft muslin and a coral necklace, while the other wore merely a coarse tow-linen shirt which barely reached to his knees, and no jewelry.

Alarmed at seeing other slaves in the family only narrowly escape being sold down the river, Roxy feels compelled to protect her child by interchanging him with his white counterpart. The slave, Chambers, grows up as the heir, Tom, while Tom grows up as Chambers, the slave and body servant of the presumed Tom. Until the conclusion of the novel when Pudd'nhead Wilson, to that point a somewhat tangential character, discerns the truth through his mastery of the new science of fingerprinting, Roxy and her son are the only ones to know of the deception.

In an essay in the *Atlantic* for July 1862, Nathaniel Hawthorne had mentioned a "historical circumstance, known to few, that connects the children of the Puritans with these Africans of Virginia in a very singular way. They are our brethren, as being lineal descendants from the Mayflower, the fated womb of which, in her first voyage, sent forth a brood of Pilgrims on Plymouth Rock, and, in a subsequent one, spawned slaves upon the Southern soil— a monstrous birth, but with which we have an instinctive sense of kindred." There is no reason to believe Twain had ever read that essay, but he conceptualized the tie between the races in similar terms. Hawthorne affirmed the unerasable natural bond between races by symbolically providing them with a common womb;

Twain did so by fictionally providing them with a common father. He dramatized the logical absurdity of the laws that insisted upon essential racial difference by showing Tom, with his inheritance restored at the novel's conclusion, incapable of exercising his newfound liberty because of a lifetime spent as a slave, while the true Chambers, who had been condemned to death for a murder he committed, has his sentence reprieved when his true identity is revealed because he is no longer a man, who has only his life to lose, but a piece of property whose death would mean financial loss to his owner—so he is sold down the river.

Throughout Twain's fictions women had been the all but stereotypical Aunt Pollys, kindly mothering, or Miss Watsons, shrewishly managing. Sharper etchings flashed forth occasionally, most memorably Mrs. Judith Loftus, who amusedly penetrates one layer of Huck Finn's disguises; but once Huck leaves the shanty he had entered only minutes before, she disappears. Prior to Roxy, the only extended exception to Twain's customary women was Laura Hawkins of *The Gilded Age*, who, having been seduced and abandoned, does not sink into despair, consumption, or death in childbirth, but accepts the lure of her sexuality and uses her charm to achieve success as a lobbyist in corrupt Washington. When she eventually encounters the seducer who had abandoned her and murders him, she is acquitted on an insanity plea, Twain thus using her as an instrument with which to lambaste a legal process he had attacked in other writings as well. Although Laura does die before the novel ends, he visits from what his point of view is an even worse punishment upon her: when she takes to the lecture platform she meets with a hostile audience.

Roxy is the most complex character in *Pudd'nhead Wilson*. Her decision initiates the plot, and her actions sustain it. No other woman in Twain's pages approximates her depth of character and attractive force. She acts from mother love but is not above black-mail to compel her son to adhere to her, and of all the characters she has the most nuanced view of racial difference and the most calculated and ironic response to it. Laura Hawkins and Roxy are both sexual transgressors, as if Twain could only reach beyond the one-dimensionality of his usual women by making them sin-ners. There were either good women or bad, and the flatness of the former was, for him, the badge of their virtue. The allure of Roxy in all her dark complexity could, it seemed, be resisted only by an almost desperate recoil toward her exaggerated opposite: the single-minded Joan in all her lily-white splendor.

Even three decades after Emancipation, Twain treads carefully in *Pudd'nhead Wilson*, never explicitly mentioning what is obvious: that the doubles have the same father. Moreover, when the plot inexorably moves toward the need for the presumed heir to mur-der the man who had propagated his and his "twin's" tragedy, Twain sidesteps and has him murder the uncle who became his guardian after his father's death. But as Leslie Fiedler persuasively argues, the logic of the book demands that the man he murders be his biological father; and, as Arlin Turner reports, manuscript notes show that Twain had once planned a scene in which the murderer hesitates to do the deed until his father pleads, "O spare me!— I am your father!" to which he responds, "Now for *that*, you shall die," and so kills him.[10] Such a scene would not have been well received by his readers, nor, perhaps, would it have been accepted by his publisher.

Still, the self-censorship is not such that the reader misses the terrible truths that are being told. In the aftermath of Reconstruc-tion, the murdered father, the aristocratic slave lord, had regained his sanctified position—see the wealth of antebellum romances—and the freedman had been returned to a servitude now inescapable since it was based on race alone rather than law. The theme Hawthorne had raised briefly was to become the burden of William Faulkner's novels, most notably *Absalom, Absalom*, the very title of which announces the doubling with which Twain is concerned in his novel. Between Hawthorne and Faulkner comes *Pudd'nhead Wilson*, the work of another American master.

Four

HUMORIST

IN THE ACCOUNT GIVEN IN "OLD TIMES ON THE MISSISSIPPI," MARK Twain left the town for the river to seek distinction. The town bred in its boys fantasies of the capture of murderers and the discovery of buried treasure, but realistically there seemed no escape from the droning slumber that enveloped all animate beings from the pigs in the street to the clerks in the stores to the people in their homes—except to take to the river.

If the town was not sufficient for the dreams of its children neither was it materially self-sufficient. It relied upon manufactured goods, marketed its agricultural products externally to acquire the capital necessary for their purchase, and was located on the river because the cost of transporting commodities on overland wagons would have been prohibitive. The daily visits of the one upriver and one downriver steamboat that called in were the central events in an otherwise humdrum existence. The boats brought goods and they brought newspapers, but beyond these services they fed the imagination: for two ten-minute periods each day they brought theater, staging a performance at each landing as the cabin boy emerged on deck to shake out tablecloths; the mate at the gangplank unfurled his mastery of the diction of execration; and, leaning out of his perch on high, the pilot perfected his nonchalant, sunburned gaze into the middle distance. The builders and owners of the steamboats supplied an aesthetic to which the town came alive, building each paddle wheeler with an arrangement of decks, stacks, and wheels specific to it so that its profile was distinctive, and decorating it to the limits of the painter's gifts. More than commerce arrived at the wharf—a sense of style came to town. The aesthetic of total efficiency awaited mass production and the railroad. The steamboat rumbling unsteadily before it into the age of steam still carried with it an insistence upon the individual peculiarity of the craftsman. Floating on the river was the eminence toward which young Mark Twain reached, and its mixture of trade, craft, and gaudy display was to influence his performance as a writer.

"Old Times" describes Twain's days as a pilot, the major part concerned with his training during his apprenticeship. He learned the shape of hundreds of miles of river downstream only to find that the knowledge had to be doubled because the upstream shape was different, and then redoubled because nighttime navigation differed from daytime. To meet the prodigious feats of memory required of him, he was forced to empty himself of all he thought he knew about the river—indeed about nature in general—a purging accomplished through his subjection to a steady stream of humiliations. Finally, at the defining point in his education, the countless details he had memorized transformed themselves from what he knew into the way he knew, what he saw into the way he saw. Quantity of knowledge became quality of perception—and he was a pilot.

Although he was speaking of piloting, when he described his emergence from apprenticeship into competence, Twain did so in the imagery of linguistic attainment: "Now when I had mastered the language of the water and had come to know every trifling feature that bordered the great river as familiarly as I knew the letters of the alphabet, I had made a valuable acquisition." In illustration he depicted a sunset scene on the river, first reading it with the innocent eye he once possessed, which led him to a "speechless rapture" at the beauty of what he beheld, then reading it with the eye of experience, recognizing that the red-gold of the sun reflected in the water meant wind tomorrow, the floating black log meant a rising river, the many-tinted break on the river's surface meant a bluff reef, and so forth. The river, in short, talked to the trained eye in terms of practical information, most of it predictive of peril, whereas the ignorant eye, deluded by the beauty of surface appearances, failed to apprehend what they signified.

The analogy between the language of nature and the language of words, the craft of the pilot and the craft of the writer, informs Twain's authorial practice. As creative writer and as critic he consistently distrusted prose that asserted the reality of such concepts as beauty or nobility simply because the words were attached to particular appearances. Reality for him consisted in apprehending the specific nature of the particular, not in labeling it. He was a literary nominalist, insisting that there was no whole larger than its named parts, no ideal larger than the details of experience, and he took unrestrained delight in caricaturing transgressors. For example, in a piece titled "A Cure for the Blues" he wrote:

> In his long-vanished day the Southern author had a passion
> for 'eloquence;' it was his pet, his darling. He would be eloquent

or perish. And he recognized only one kind of eloquence, the lurid, the tempestuous, the volcanic. He liked words; big words, fine words, grand words, rumbling, thundering, reverberating words—with sense attaching to it if it could be got in without marring the sound but not otherwise.

In Twain's view no reality invoked by writing could be greater than the syntax and diction employed in its composition, and while he took some enjoyment in recalling the empty verbiage of the southern author of the vanished past, he was in righteous ire when he attacked Sir Walter Scott's fictions as the pernicious source of much of what he found wrong with postwar southern culture. Scott "with his enchantments," he said, "and by his single might checks the wave of progress, and even turns it back; sets the world in love with dreams and phantoms; with decayed and swinish forms of religion; with decayed and degraded systems of government; with the silliness and emptiness, sham grandeurs, sham gauds, and sham chivalries of a brainless and worthless long-vanished society." Although most of the world had outgrown him, in the South "the genuine and wholesome civilization of the nineteenth century is curiously confused and commingled with the Walter Scott Middle-Age sham civilization, and so you have practical common-sense, progressive ideas, and progressive works, mixed up with the duel, the inflated speech, and the jejune romanticism of an absurd past that is dead, and out of charity ought to be buried." In *Huckleberry Finn* there is a derelict steamboat on which villains plot murder before being swept away and drowned when the wreck sinks in a storm. The boat's name is *Walter Scott*.

James Fenimore Cooper, the "American Scott" as he was often called, was the subject of Twain's fullest and most trenchant attack on the kind of foggy prose that was taken to signify something but in fact blurred all meaning. In "Fenimore Cooper's Literary Offenses" he scolded the influential critics who had praised Cooper's *Leatherstocking Tales*, pointing out to them Cooper's clumsy handling of dialogue, his insipid characterizations, and the flat-out impossibility of the achievements he claimed for his hero. Most importantly, he focused on Cooper's language, measuring its shortcomings against a concise set of rules that governed good writing:

> The author shall
> *Say* what he is proposing to say, not merely come near it.
> Use the right word, not its second cousin.
> Eschew surplusage.
> Not omit necessary details.
> Avoid slovenliness of form.
> Use good grammar.
> Employ a simple and straightforward style.

The clear implication was that if Cooper's prose had followed these precepts, in being more precise it would also have made impossible most of the episodes that made up his plots. Truth to life cannot emerge from bad grammar and directionless syntax.

Admirers of Cooper might reply that despite his faulty prose, a developing sense of the ambiguity of the American experience broods over his pages as his hero flees westward, away from society's wasteful invasion of nature, only to find himself opening a path for that society's further invasion of nature. The great scenes in the novels, it might be argued, are not episodes of adventure so much as they are symbolic moments impregnated with conflicting cultural claims and, as such, rise above the incidental irregularities of the prose. But Twain would not receive such an argument kindly. For him no fictive reality can be greater than the syntax and diction employed in its composition.

Even as it strengthened his actualization of separate scenes, Twain's literary nominalism, his belief that no reality exists apart from particulars, contributed to the structural weakness of his longer fictions. He was ever vulnerable to the attraction of specific episodes without regard to their effect on the theme of the work as a whole. But it is also the source of his great and distinctive power, and of the sanative influence he exerted upon modern American literature, turning it to the right word rather than its modifiers, and to the avoidance of undocumented generalizations.

Eve, in Twain's sketch, "Eve's Diary" (1906), assigns names to the newly created animals she sees in accordance with what they look like; she names them, that is, after their kind: "The minute I set eyes on an animal I know what it is. I don't have to reflect a moment; the right name comes out instantly, just as if it were an inspiration, as no doubt it is, for I am sure it wasn't in me half a minute before. I seem to know just by the shape of the creature and the way it acts what animal it is." The Bible assigns such naming to Adam—"whatsoever the man called every living creature, that was the name thereof"—but Twain gives the task to Eve because his Adam is too busy setting mankind on a shaky verbal journey as he ostentatiously unfurls words such as "superfluous," "judicious," and "enigma."

After God created the world He left it to humans to complete the creation by making the objects in the world available to thought through attaching words to them. Right naming—seeing that "elephant" is the correct word to assign to the enormous pachyderm and "ant" is not—is, therefore, essential. The fable of the nonarbitrary nature of words, one that informs much of poetic discourse, guides the spirit of Twain's nominalism as well.

When Twain in his critical writings analyzes a writer's composition in terms of the precision demanded by the set of rules by which he measured Cooper, he is, in effect, applying a literary lie detector. To identify imprecise diction and careless syntax is to expose untruths in what the writing presumes to assert. For him the form was inseparable from the material of which it was made. A written work was not verbal, made up of words, so much as it was the words themselves. In *Roughing It*, for example, after some predictable joking about the constitution of polygamous households in Salt Lake City, he offered his considered appraisal of Mormonism through a detailed critique of passages from its sacred writings. What struck his ear as hollow locutions dressed up in a shoddy imitation of biblical diction indicated to him the shallowness of the beliefs founded on it.

Likewise, his distrust of Christian Science was based on his observation of the faults in Mary Baker Eddy's prose. One Eddy sentence began, for example, "Naturally, my first jottings were but efforts to express in feeble diction Truth's ultimate . . ." Twain comments, "One understands what she means, but she should have been able to say what she meant—if she had put 'feeble' in front of 'efforts' and then left out 'in' and 'diction' she would have scored." Minor, even trivial, as such a correction might appear to be, it actually takes us to the heart of Twain's emphasis upon language as, in Gary Wills's phrase, "the indicator of mental and moral conditions."[1]

When Mary Baker Eddy wrote, "No one else can drain the cup which I have drunk to the dregs, as the discoverer and teacher of Christian Science," Mark Twain replied:

That is saying we cannot empty an empty cup. We knew it before; and we know she meant to tell us that particular cup is going to remain empty. That is, we think that that was the idea, but we cannot be sure. She has a perfectly astonishing talent for putting words together in such a way as to make successful inquiry into their intention impossible.

In another context, however, such a talent for obfuscation was one of the hallmarks of Twain's humor. He delighted in what he described as " a string of plausibly worded sentences that didn't mean anything under the sun." It was a kind of verbal equivalent to the practical joke with all of the practical joker's straight-faced luring of its victim into the trap but with none of its cruelty. The listener is drawn into a discourse that promises to yield meaning—even useful information—as plausible sentence succeeds plausible sentence, only to awaken slowly to the realization that the sum total is sheer nonsense. Although Twain was given to crediting Artemus Ward with the perfection of this technique, one more than suspects that his alleged quotation of Ward is actually his own construction. Here is Twain's account of the question that Ward asked him about silver mining as he repeated it in "First Interview with Artemus Ward":

> Now, what I want to get at is—is, well, the way the deposits of ore are made you know. For instance. Now as I understand it, the vein which contains the silver is sandwiched in between casings of granite, and runs along the ground, and sticks up like a curbstone. Well, take a vein of forty feet thick, for example, or eighty, for that matter, or even a hundred—say you go down five hundred feet, or maybe you don't go down but two hundred—anyway you go down, and all the time the vein grows narrower when the casings

come nearer or approach each other, you may say—that is, when they do approach, which of course they do not always do, particularly in cases where the nature of the formation is such that they stand wider apart, wider than they otherwise would, and which geology has failed to account for, although everything in that science goes to prove that, all things being equal, it would if it did not, or would certainly if it did, and then of course they are. Do you think it is?

What emerges from this passage is the sheer pleasure Twain takes in the lubricity of language that can so subtly spin speaker and listener out from any perceptible reality and into the comic realm of nonsense. This is the same capacity of language that in other contexts he exposes as having abetted dishonesty, which is to say that just as Twain's satires on human folly are the obverse side of the doctrine of original sin, so his joy in the elaborate muddle that mere language can create is the obverse side of his condemnation of the moral ruin it can wreak. The many comic changes that he rings on the theme of language's lubricity are assigned to speaking voices, whereas language's potential for damage almost always resides in a more formalized written language, or in speech that consciously strains for literary effect. Ursula K. Le Guinn observes that Twain's "indestructible prose" is that of a living person speaking, and adds, "I wonder if this is why we trust him, even though he lets us down so often."[2]

"There are several kinds of stories," Twain wrote, "but only one difficult kind—the humorous. . . . The humorous story depends for its effect upon the *manner* of the telling; the comic story and the witty story upon the *matter*." Taken very loosely the distinction appears valid, although once one comes to examples the lines begin to blur. Still, it is clear that Twain's humor resides in the manner of telling, and that the teller best suited for the task is one who is ostensibly serious and unaware of the humorous dimension of what he is saying. Contrasting with the laughable statements he makes, his sober, often pedantic, manner enhances the humorous effect of the content of his conversation.

In Twain's earliest writings the speaker was very much the grave idiot exemplified by Ward raising his question about mining. But as he progressed he refined such speakers until in Huck Finn he had one who was unaware that he was behaving admirably rather than immorally when he disobeyed the inhumane conventions of his society—the inspired idiot transformed into undesigning satirist. Whether the speaker was idiot, satirist, or something in between, in Twain's tales the humor depended always on the teller's possession of a character distinctly fitted to the tale he told. Whereas the wit and the comic, always conscious of the laughter they aim to provoke, are essentially the same at each appearance, Twain's tellers differ from each other in accordance with the matter of their tale.

Today Mark Twain's place in American literature rests on his novels, but, as Judith Yaross Lee has noted, "he built his nineteenth-century reputation and his literary technique on comic journalism."[3] That reputation, moreover, was elaborated through his constant presence in newspapers and magazines as subject as well as author, and his frequent appearances at banquets and other public affairs. No American writer before or since has occupied so large a space in the public mind, and his presence there seems, finally, to be larger than the sum of what he wrote or said—ironically so, in view of his insistence that in literary matters there is no reality other than the sum of the particulars.

Although after his death Twain's reputation receded into the pages of his books, some sense of his living presence may still be glimpsed in the letters and sketches that throughout his life he threw off, as it were, at the spur of the moment. Here, for example, is Mark Twain in 1872, the year in which his first novel was published. A portrait of William Dean Howells had recently appeared in the magazine *Hearth & Home*, and in June he writes to Howells:

> Bret Harte has been here & says his family would not be without that portrait for any consideration. He says his children get up in the night & yell for it. I would give anything for a copy of that portrait to put in my parlor. I have Oliver Wendell Holmes's & Bret Harte's, as published in Every Saturday, & of all the swarms that come every day to gaze upon them none go away that are not softened & humbled & made more resigned to the will of God. If I had yours to put up alongside of them, I believe the combination would bring more souls to earnest reflection & ultimate conviction of their lost condition than any other kind of warning would. Where in the nation *can* I get that portrait? There is my uncle. *He* wants a copy. He is lying at the point of death. He has *been* lying at the point of death for two years. He wants a copy—& I want him to *have* a copy. And I want you to send a copy to the man that shot my dog. I want to see if he is dead to every human instinct.[4]

Fifteen years later he is petitioning Queen Victoria. The Inland Revenue office, mistakenly believing he was to take up residence in England, had levied an income tax upon his English royalties, and he has decided to sort the matter out by writing to her, he explains, rather than to Edward Bright, the clerk of the Inland Revenue who had notified him of the tax, because

> I do not know Mr. Bright, and it is embarrassing to me to correspond with strangers, for I was raised in the country and have always lived there, the early part in Marion County, Missouri, before the war, and this part in Hartford County, Connecticut, near Bloomfield and about 8 miles this side of Farmington, though some call it 9, which it is impossible to be, for I have walked it many and many a time in considerably under three hours and General Hawley says he has done it in two and a quarter, which is not likely; so it has seemed best that I write your Majesty.

Although he has never met her, he says, he had once met her son in London when he was on top of an omnibus in Oxford Street when Prince Edward passed heading a procession. The Prince would likely remember him because of the gray coat with flap pockets that he wore; no one else on the omnibus wore the same kind of coat. He calls Queen Victoria's attention to the fact that Schedule D under which he is taxed includes "Trades, Offices, and Gas Works," and since he does not regard authorship as a trade and does not have an office he does not believe himself taxable under that Schedule—the reader is left to ponder his omission of "Gas Works."—and therefore asks that his publisher not be required to withhold tax money from his royalties: "You will not miss the sum, but this is a hard year for authors, and as for lectures I do not suppose your Majesty ever saw such a dull season."[5]

Both of the speakers in these examples are familiar to those who have read Twain's better-known works where such types are also to be found. Yet appearing in these less familiar writings they suggest to today's reader, as his novels do not, how Twain was perceived by the public during his lifetime. His was a being that constantly manifested itself in writings—even his letters seem to have been written with a readership larger than the recipient in mind—yet was never embodied by them. His many appearances in print were the manifestations of a spirit apart from them. Twain's inability to arrive at a finished form in his longer works contributed to this sense of him as an uncontainable force that could burst forth at any moment regardless of context; as an artificer apart from his creations rather than an architect of larger structures that, in effect, embodied him. In this respect, Theodore Dreiser, whose novels began to appear ten years before Twain's death, seems his direct opposite: a somber writer, clumsy in his phrasing and awkward in his syntax, from whose inexorable massing of the sticks and stones of life a terrible new world emerges.

A Connecticut Yankee was published in 1889 on the eve of a decade that saw the rise in America of the naturalistic novel in which individual will was portrayed as powerless in the face of impersonal forces, social as well as natural. The movement of population from the homogeneous communities of the countryside into socially disunified communities concentrated in the cities, the growth of a labor force stripped of individuality by the techniques of mass production, and the scientific recognition of the role of biological impulses in human behavior all contributed to shape the plots of Frank Norris (born 1870), Stephen Crane (born 1871), and Theodore Dreiser (born 1871). Crane's Maggie and Dreiser's Carrie each entered upon what was conventionally regarded as a "life of sin," compelled by social forces beyond their control: Maggie to her ruin and Carrie to her personal advancement. Both women, Maggie in New York living with a drunken mother in a slum tenement and country-bred Carrie adrift in clamorous Chicago, work in factories for wages that will never advance them beyond the sordidness of their daily existence. Carrie is offered a choice between continuing her career as a commodity on the unskilled labor market, a virgin with cheap boots through which the snow penetrates as she tramps the windswept streets, or submitting to the desires of her would-be lover and becoming a woman whose virginity has been lost but whose clothes are weatherproof and apartment heated. Maggie's circumstances are not identical, but they are analogous.

Twain's Laura and his Roxy also were seduced—in Roxy's slave condition it might, perhaps, better be said "coerced." Yet as much as he scorns the seducers—both, strikingly, Southern "gentlemen"—and although Laura's initial condition is, like Maggie's, that of trusting innocence while Roxy's literal slavery somewhat parallels Carrie's wage slavery, Twain holds both women responsible for their deeds. In the naturalistic novel the actions of the women are neither condemned nor admired because blame and praise can only attach to actions that arise from the operation of free will. When Carrie yields to the propositions of her seducer she is responding to the desperation of her condition in a city whose forces overwhelm her, and Dreiser simply asks, without himself answering, what it is that she has lost by yielding.

Yet Twain was far from disagreeing with a determinist philosophy that denied free will. After reading Elinor Glyn's novel *Three Weeks* (1907), in which sexual passion is regarded as sacred and so justifies the violation of the conventions of sexual propriety, he said, "The unstated argument of the book is that the laws of Nature are paramount and properly take precedence of the interfering and impertinent restrictions obtruded upon man's life and man's statutes." He accepted Glyn's point, and when she visited him had a frank talk with her about the hypocrisy of the sexual mores of the day, but he refused her request that he publicly endorse her book, saying that although the laws of Nature were the laws of God, "we must steadfastly refuse to obey those laws, and we must as steadfastly stand by the conventions which ignore them, since the statutes furnish us peace, fairly good government, and stability, and therefore are better for us than the laws of God."[6] For the naturalists, however, it was not a matter of whether the laws of nature were to be obeyed, but rather that it was not possible to disobey them.

Twain's certainty that humans were not free agents increased throughout the 1890s but was not prominent in any of the stories and sketches he published in the ten collections that appeared between the 1894 publication of *Pudd'nhead Wilson* and his death in 1910. The most prominent exception would seem to be the story, "The Man That Corrupted Hadleyburg," in which an entire community that prides itself on its unimpeachable moral stature is powerless to resist dishonesty when the opportunity for riches is dangled before it. To some extent this may be called a work of naturalism, although its principal theme would appear to be that virtue untested is not virtue at all. More relevant to that theme than naturalism is a sketch titled "My First Lie and How I Got Out of It" (1899), in which Twain discussed spoken lies that are condemned as opposed to the unspoken ones that remain unchallenged beneath a facade of virtue. Slavery in America, the treatment of Dreyfus in France, the English manufacture of a war in South Africa were all based, he said, on "The silent assertion that nothing is going on which fair and intelligent men are aware of and are engaged by their duty to try to stop. . . . When whole races and peoples conspire to propagate gigantic mute lies in the interest of tyrannies and shams, why should we care anything about the trifling lies told by individuals?" The sketch was published in book form in the collection that included "The Man That Corrupted Hadleyburg" and goes further to illuminate that story than does an application of the theory of naturalism. If it resembles that of any writer of the 1890s, Twain's theme of communal hypocrisy, the capacity of an entire society to live and enforce a lie, the writer is Henrik Ibsen.

In early 1902 his close friend, the Reverend Joseph Twichell, lent Mark Twain a copy of Jonathan Edwards's 1754 treatise, *Freedom of Will*. The morning after he read the work, Twain said in a letter to Twichell, he rose "with a strange & haunting sense of having been on a three days' tear with a drunken lunatic." Edwards's was, he said, "a resplendent intellect gone mad." But having thus dissociated himself from any affinity with Edwards's religiosity, he went on to say that Edwards seems to hold

> that the man (or his soul or his will) never *creates* an impulse itself, but is moved to action by an impulse back of it. That's sound! Also, that of two or more things offered it, it infallibly chooses the one which for the moment is most *pleasing* to IT-SELF. *Perfectly* correct!

He continued in the letter to point up his agreements with Edwards's theology—although curiously framing them as if he had preceded the eighteenth-century minister so that Edwards was acceding to *his* positions—and then said that this being so, it was time for Edwards "to get alarmed," because "he was pointed straight for the only rational & possible next station on *that* piece of road, the irresponsibility of man to God."[7] But Edwards shirked this "next station" on his logical path, retreating behind the doctrine of predestination that holds that some humans have been ordained from the beginning of time to be saved and thus can be comfortable with the fact that most men are damned. Twain, however, does not accept this escape from the determinism he shares with Edwards. "I believe," he wrote in another piece, "that only one command has ever been issued and that command was issued in the beginning of time, in the first second of time; that command resulted in an act, in Adam's first act—if there was an Adam—and that from that act sprang another act as natural and unavoidable consequence, let us say it was Eve's act—and that from *that* act proceeded *another* act of one of these two persons as an unavoidable consequence; and now the chain of natural and unavoidable happenings being started there has never been a break in it from that day to this."[8] For Twain the whole human race is damned, or, what comes to the same thing, if there is a god he is a cruel god and man owes him nothing.

From the 1890s until his death in 1910 Twain certainly had grounds for his dismay at the human condition. At the age of sixty he saw himself a bankrupt having to work his way back to solvency; and in his consequent lecture tour around the world, he witnessed the injustices visited upon whole populations in Southeast Asia, Australia, and Africa by colonial exploiters who defended their invasions as the introduction of Christianity and material progress to benighted peoples. Returning from the tour he found the Spanish-American War, which he had hailed as one of liberation for the people of the Philippines, modulating into American entry into the nefarious fraternity of colonial powers as the Philippine nationalists were violently suppressed. And domestically he underwent the torment of the death of his favorite daughter, Susy, from spinal meningitis in 1896, an anguish renewed by the death of his wife Livy in 1904, and, in the same year, the collapse and medical confinement of his second daughter, Clara, and the diagnosis of his third daughter, Jean, who was to die the year before he himself did, as epileptic. His private comments in those decades were terrible cries of pain. In a letter to Howells after Susy's death, for example, he scorned the consolation offered by the doctrine of life after death: "And shall we see Susy? Without doubt! without *shadow* of doubt, if it can furnish opportunity to break our hearts again."[9]

But that bitterness was not apparent in the essentially humorous writings he continued to produce. So far as his publications were concerned, his ire was confined, in the main, to polemical political writings in which he attacked the monstrous practices of the colonial powers, the United States among them. When his bitterness does uncontrollably burst forth in nonpolemical writings, however, it is, in its extremity, fearful to behold—the cry of a bounteous spirit that has been wounded to the quick. So when in *Following the Equator* he is shown a lignified caterpillar with a plant growing out of the back of its neck, "a ghastly curiosity," he bursts forth:

No caterpillar can deceive Nature. If this one couldn't suffer Nature would have known it, and would have hunted up another caterpillar. Not that she would have let this one go, merely because it was defective. No. She would have waited and let him turn into a night-moth; and then fried him in the candle.

The grounds for his pessimism were broad. And yet pessimism is not necessarily determinism, and when he published his one extended exposition of his determinist philosophy "What Is Man" (1906), he said in his introductory note that his studies for the papers that made up the book began twenty-five years earlier. Mark Twain, who was ever drawn to the acquaintanceship of ministers, was also ever drawn to theology as the intellectual frame that best encompassed his philosophy. In this respect he was very much a nineteenth-century American, framing answers to questions of life in terms of mankind's relation to the deity.

From 1884 into the following year, the *Century Magazine* ran an extremely popular series of reminiscences titled *Battles and Leaders of the Civil War*. When the magazine's editor heard Twain tell of his brief wartime experience with an irregular band of the Confederate militia, he urged him to write about it, and the memoir "The Private History of a Campaign That Failed" appeared in the December 1885 issue of the magazine. It was an account of the two weeks of inept military preparation Twain spent with a group of poorly organized fellow townsmen after the war had closed down traffic on the Mississippi—and with it his profession as a pilot. Two weeks of playing soldier were enough, and he eagerly seized the opportunity to join his brother Orion on the journey to Nevada that eventuated in a career in journalism and the creation of Mark Twain.

"The Private History of a Campaign That Failed" is curiously, even nervously, mixed in tone, a humorous account of bumbling amateurs playing at war. None accepts any rank below officer, and all glow in the admiration of their neighbors; the story ends somberly as the "soldiers" blindly shoot in the dark at a supposed enemy and then creep up to his fallen body to find that he is at the point of death. The dying man was not armed and was not in uniform, and it seemed, Twain wrote, that before dying the man gave him a reproachful look and muttered about his wife and child. He may have been a spy—he may not—but all that could be learned of him was that he was a stranger in the country: "I could not drive it away, the taking of that unoffending life seemed such a wanton thing. And it seemed an epitome of war; that all war must be just that—the killing of strangers against whom you feel no personal animosity; strangers whom in other circumstances you would help if you found them in trouble, and who would help you if you needed it." Sam Clemens's war was over, and Mark Twain's life was about to begin. Forrest G. Robinson, commenting on this, says: "In putting on his new identity, the young man was also groping for a new way of escaping the humiliating failure that lay behind him in wartime Missouri." He cites James Cox's contention that "the humorous identity and personality of 'Mark Twain' was a grand evasion of the Civil War."[10]

Twain's "Private History" exudes its author's uneasiness at having taken part in the episode and then not going on to participate in the war. By the time he wrote it Twain was a celebrated fixture at the banquets of the Grand Army of the Republic and other veterans' groups. He regarded Ulysses S. Grant as the greatest American of his time, valued his friendship immensely, and was, famously, to rescue Grant's family from the straitened circumstances that threatened his wife and children. Twain contracted to publish Grant's *Memoirs* on financial terms that left the family in comfortable circumstances (Grant had died shortly after completing his *Memoirs*). Other reminiscences in the *Century* series were those of recognized heroes, and Civil War histories and memoirs dominated the list of subscription books issued by Twain's publisher. The war reached into every American home while it was being waged and touched every American village for decades after its ending, with a monument to the townsmen who had fought erected on every green, North and South. Daily one could see men on the street or in the fields still wearing one or another item of clothing left over from their military kits; fireside talk turned time and again to where one was and what one did during the war; veterans' reunions and encampments occurred annually; and throughout the century military service during the war was an implicit prerequisite for political office, including the presidency. For those who had lived through the war years, either on or off the battlefield, the memory of it was sacred—in the North of a holy war to end slavery and preserve the Union; in the South of the martyrdom suffered to preserve a way of life that must now be kept alive by never forgetting the way it used to be.

Manifestly uneasy at his own war record, Twain chose to place his decidedly antiheroic memoir in the *Century* series beside those of men who had fought bravely so that, having made his confession of foolish boyhood posturing and its fatal consequence, he was, then, freed from having to shy away from invitations to speak at memorial banquets. In such talks he frequently reprised the details of his *Century* memoir, concentrating on the humor rather than the fatal episode at its end. But while his brief period in the militia band can be documented from other sources, no amount of assiduous research has been able to uncover the shooting incident of which he wrote. It appears to be fictitious, and the reader is left to conjecture as to why he needed to create and perhaps even to believe it. And why did he represent himself as so adolescently naive when, in point of fact, he was at the time an experienced twenty-six-year-old riverboat pilot? Even as the piece served to validate his entry into the companionship of those who fought in the war, it was a parable of youth and disillusionment that justified his flight from it, a difficult two-way feat to accomplish, but, judging from the piece's popularity, one that succeeded.

In 1895, ten years after the publication of the "Private History," Stephen Crane's *Red Badge of Courage* appeared—to widespread acclaim. Born after the war, Crane had received his impressions of it from conversations with veterans as well as reading the *Battles and Leaders* series. His protagonist, identified throughout as the "Youth," enlists in the Union army with romantic dreams of glory, only to find himself one in a mass of nameless and often faceless men ignorant of where they are or why they are moving in whatever direction they are ordered to move. In this mental fog, accentuated by the smoke of gunpowder and the darkness of night marches, the Youth is governed by impulses starker than words—his thoughts pathetic rationalizations after the fact, never reflections that lead to decisions and deeds. The affirmative reception the book received brought to the surface veterans' acknowledgments that, whatever the leaders and the historians might say, their experience of war was an experience of fear, uncertainty, and so deep an immersion in the particulars of camping, fighting, retreating, advancing, and, above all, waiting, that they lost sense of any relationship to a larger scheme or purpose. When *The Red Badge of Courage* appeared Twain was beginning his round-the-world tour, after which he settled in London to write his travel book, moved on to Vienna, and then back to London. But the popularity of Crane's novel was so great and Twain's correspondent, Howells, so admired it, that he could not have escaped encountering its reputation, if not the novel itself.[11] In its pages he would have found the explicit assertion of war's murderous erasure of all reason that he, being of the war generation, could only express, and that timorously, by providing a fictionalized killing appended to a "humorous" sketch.

"On October 15, 1900," Justin Kaplan writes, "Mark Twain returned to America and to an ovation that went on for the rest of his life."[12]

Although in the remaining ten years of his life he was to be tormented by the illnesses of family members and the deaths of his wife and daughter Jean, although he was deeply disturbed in those years by the atrocities committed by King Leopold's regime in the Congo and the desperate condition of millions in Russia under the tyrannous conduct of their monarchy, and although he then crystallized his ideas about the "damned" human race, he nevertheless also responded heartily to the ovation, not only basking in the loving admiration of his countrymen but playing to it. Albert Bigelow Paine, his neighbor, companion, and aide in his last years, said in his biography, "Mark Twain was not a pessimist in his heart, but only by premeditation. It was his observation and his logic that led him to write these things that, even in their bitterness, somehow conveyed that spirit of human sympathy that is so closely linked to hope."[13] There is more than a touch of a devotee's pious glossing in the remark. But while the "hope" that he attributes to Twain at his darkest may be wishful thinking, nevertheless it is also evident that Twain's philosophical dismay rarely if ever interfered with his zestful response to the esteem in which he was held. It was in the years of the lasting ovation that he adopted the habit of wearing a suit of white in all seasons, saying, however, that if it was at all feasible he would have preferred wearing his Oxford doctoral gown at all times. Physically drained as he sometimes was, he continued to accept invitations to speak to student groups, literary gatherings, and commemorative banquets, and to appear, even when he did not speak, at gatherings on behalf of one or another worthy cause. Such occasions cheered his spirit even when they sapped his stamina. In New York for one such event, he was staying at the Waldorf Astoria when Paine, seeking to conserve Twain's strength by shielding him from intrusive encounters, led him to the banquet room by a private way, only to have Twain insist that they go back upstairs in order for him to enjoy returning by way of the grand staircase in full sight of the public.

Immediately after the Civil War American literary magazines featured what were called "local color" stories in which the characters and incidents depicted could only have existed in the specific locales in which the stories were set. It was as if—with the Union now safely preserved—it was permissible to take delight in the many different regional and ethnic cultures that made up the nation. Differences no longer threatened to be divisive but became parts of the wonderful kaleidoscope of folkways that made up American life. George Washington Cable's Louisiana Cajuns, Joel Chandler Harris's Uncle Remus, and Bret Harte's Californians, among others, seized the public imagination, and Twain's "Jumping Frog" as well, owed some of their celebrity to the popular appeal of local color. The genre can also be credited with the first wide entry of women into the literary marketplace since an emphasis on regional habits warranted an emphasis on domestic manners, and women whose themes were eventually to extend well beyond the depiction of household manners gained an entry by way of such regionalism: Mary Wilkins Freeman and Sarah Orne Jewett from New England, for example, or Kate Chopin from New Orleans.

Although Twain's literary career initially marked him as a regional writer, and although his major fictions centered in the region of his boyhood, he rose to fame as the quintessentially American writer—the writer whose work most recognizably represented the national character. He was cherished by readers in all sections of the nation; while in the aftermath of Lincoln's death sectional frictions remained inflammable, his achievement rose above the divisiveness. Lee and Grant were the heroes of sectional cultures; Mark Twain, preeminently the hero of a national culture. Speaking of the label "Mark Twain," James Cox said, "The very pen name implies the presence of a division, it neither denotes nor requires one and can equally be seen as a means of containing the very division it marks."[14]

The greatest of all the divisions contained, that is reconciled, by this author, who was so often fascinated by the phenomenon of twinning or doubling, was that of sectionalism. He was a southerner by birth and a northerner by residence, but above all in his arrival in the East from California he was a westerner, and whereas in the national imagination North was North and South was South, the West was America. It was, Hawthorne once remarked, that portion of the nation over which the damned shadow of Europe had not fallen. It was, as political orators unstintingly asserted, the site of the expansive future of the nation, not just in the richness of its natural resources but in the self-sufficient hardiness it bred in its inhabitants. Sudden as it was, Mark Twain's entry into literary prominence also seemed to have been long expected; it was the arrival of the western, which was to say, the American, writer.

At the core of Twain's unifying appeal is humor. As Bernard De Voto justly asserted, criticism that ignores it is absurd.[15] That Twain was first and foremost a humorist was the reason for Matthew Arnold's disdain and a frequent source of uneasiness for Twain himself because he knew he was more than a humorist. Thomas Hardy asked Howells: "Why don't people understand that Mark Twain is not merely a great humorist? He is a very remarkable fellow in a different way."[16] Yet the faintly apologetic "merely," designed to enlarge Twain's stature, actually diminishes it. His humor was what made him a very remarkable fellow indeed. "His great charm," Howells wrote, "is his absolute freedom in a region where most of us are fettered and shackled by immemorial convention. He saunters out into the trim world of letters, and lounges across its neatly kept paths, and walks about on the grass at will, in spite of all the signs that have been put up from the beginning of literature, warning people of dangers and penalties for the slightest trespass."[17]

George Ade, born in 1866, grew up in rural Indiana in a home in which subscription books were the sole literature: "distended, diluted, and altogether tasteless volumes that had been used for several decades to balance the ends of the center table," keeping company with the high-priced Bible.[18] With a dull sense of fore-

boding the boy approached the newest subscription acquisition—
it, too, thick and heavily emblazoned with gold—and found that
into the company of the other ponderous volumes crowded with
woodcuts, stuffed with commonplace pieties, and varnished with
lachrymose sentiments had crept a comic travel narrative peppered
with absurd incidents, impious observations, and a range of
characters whose ignorance and sublimely idiotic behavior were
both intensely familiar to every common American, yet had never
before been encountered in print. The pompous bores and inspired fools he—that is, every common American— met in his
everyday life were as much the stuff of literature as were exem-
plary children and monitory elders, and to laugh at all of them
was not only alright but actually unavoidable.

In page after page of Twain's writings—travel books, novels,
sketches, and stories—we encounter people whose reality is immediate. They may arrive in a brief episode and depart from the
narrative forever at the episode's conclusion, but they are instantly
and unforgettably familiar, inhabitants of the world we inhabit
outside of the book's pages: the undertaker who had no more smile
to him than a ham; the childless woman who knows that Huck is
lying to her, but silently discerning the boy's desperation, says to
him, "If you get into trouble you send word to me, Mrs. Judith
Loftus, which is me, and I'll do what I can to get you out of it" (try
putting that grammatically without destroying its simple decency);
the snobbish young fop met on shipboard—"His hair was short
and parted accurately in the middle, and he had the look of an
American person who would be likely to begin his signature with
an initial, and spell his middle name out"; the man who could never
remember anything without remembering everything so that his
stories never came to an end; the simple hay farmer who suddenly

acquired wealth through mining stock, traveled abroad, and returned to report on the marvels of European civilization—"He was never tired of telling about the fine hogs he had seen in England, and the gorgeous sheep he had seen in Spain, and the fine cattle he had noticed in the vicinity of Rome."

These and countless more of Twain's creations we had seen in life before we saw them in print but did not realize what we were seeing until he placed them before us. Now recognizing their presence in our life we see life itself differently. Literature can effect no higher end.

NOTES

CHAPTER ONE

1. Walter Licht, *Industrializing America* (Baltimore: Johns Hopkins University Press, 1995), p. 102.
2. Albert Bigelow Paine, *Mark Twain, A Biography* (New York: Harper & Brothers, 1912), 2: 879. Unless otherwise indicated, this three-volume set is the source for details of Twain's life.
3. Louis J. Budd, *Mark Twain, Social Philosopher* (Bloomington: Indiana University Press, 1962), p. 146.
4. Joel Porte, ed., *Emerson in His Journals* (Cambridge, Mass.: Harvard University Press, 1982), p. 465.
5. See the editor's foreword to Mark Twain, *No. 44, The Mysterious Stranger* (Berkeley: University of California Press, 1982) for an explanation of the "editorially fabricated" nature of earlier works that passed as *The Mysterious Stranger* by Mark Twain and the authenticity of this version. The print shop was not a feature of the fabricated versions.
6. "The Killing of Julius Caesar 'Localized,'" was published in 1869 and first appeared in book form in *Sketches, New and Old* (1875).
7. Mark Twain, *Life on the Mississippi* (New York: Oxford University Press, 1996), p. 246. This is a facsimile of the first edition of 1883.
8. Paine, *Mark Twain, A Biography*, 1:25n.
9. Ibid., 2:222.
10. *Artemus Ward His Book* (New York: Carleton Publishers, 1866), p.1.
11. *Mark Twain Speaking*, ed. Paul Fatout (Iowa City: University of Iowa Press, 1976), pp. 606–607.
12. *Mark Twain-Howells Letters*, 2 vols., ed. Henry Nash Smith and William H. Gibson (Cambridge, Mass.: Harvard University Press, 1960), 2:735.
13. Bernard De Voto, *Mark Twain's America* (Boston: Little, Brown, and Company, 1932), p. 321.
14. Paine, *Mark Twain, A Biography*, 1:242.
15. De Voto, *Mark Twain's America*, p. 138.

16. Ibid., p. viii.
17. *Mark Twain Speaking*, p. 44. Without attribution, Twain reused Ward's remark in altered form in *The Gilded Age* (1873).
18. Paine, *Mark Twain, A Biography*, 1:278.
19. *Mark Twain Speaking*, p. 44.
20. I rely on S. I. Hayakawa and Howard Mumford Jones's "Introduction" to the volume of selections from Holmes published in the American Writers Series (New York: American Book Company, 1939), and the quotations from Holmes are to be found in this edition.
21. Paine, *Mark Twain, A Biography*, 1:382.
22. See Kenneth S. Lynn, *Mark Twain and Southwest Humor* (Boston: Little Brown, 1959) for an extended, perhaps overextended, discussion of the subject.
23. Quoted in the introductory note to the story in the anthology *The First West*, ed. Edward Watts and David Rachels (New York: Oxford University Press, 2002), pp. 234–35. Faulkner, of course, did not try to rewrite it but, aware of its strengths, took another tack, one that nevertheless reflected the mythic quality of Thorpe's theme.
24. Quoted in John Henry Raleigh, *Mark Twain and American Culture* (Berkeley: University of California Press, 1957), p. 22 where the quoted lines from T. S. Eliot's "Cousin Nancy" serve as epigraph.
25. Paine, *Mark Twain, A Biography*, 2:758, 759.
26. Matthew Arnold, *Civilization in the United States* (Boston: DeWolfe, Fiske & Co., 1888), p. 92.
27. Ibid., p. 177.
28. "License of the Press," *The Complete Essays of Mark Twain*, ed. Charles Neider (Garden City: Doubleday & Company, 1963), p. 11.
29. *Mark Twain in Eruption*, ed. Bernard De Voto (New York: Harper & Brothers, 1940), p. 202.
30. *Mark Twain Speaking*, pp. 141, 142.
31. *Twain-Howells Letters*, 1:107.
32. Advertisement in the endpapers of the American Publishing Company edition of Twain's *The Innocents Abroad* (1869).
33. Paine, *Mark Twain, A Biography*, 2:895.

CHAPTER TWO

1. The discussion of Twain as a travel writer relies upon material that appeared in Chapter 4 of my *Return Passages* (New Haven: Yale University Press, 2000), some of which is reprinted here in revised form by permission of the publisher.

2. "I smiled at the conceit when I first wrote it, but when I thought how sad hearted and how full of dreams of a happier time the poor fellow might have been who scribbled it here, there was a touching pathos about it that I had never suspected it possessed before," *Mark Twain's Travels with Mr. Brown*, ed. Franklin Walker & Ezra Dane (New York: Alfred A. Knopf, 1940), p. 190.

3. Ibid., p. 136.

4. Ibid., p. 106

5. Ibid., p. 85

6. Ibid., p. 239

7. *The Adams-Jefferson Letters*, ed. Lester J. Cappon (Chapel Hill: University of North Carolina Press, 1959), 2:502.

8. Quoted in James S. Leonard's afterword to *A Tramp Abroad* (New York: Oxford University Press, 1996), p. 12.

9. Paine, *Mark Twain, A Biography*, 1:533.

10. Quoted in Richard Bridgman, *Traveling in Mark Twain* (Berkeley: University of California Press, 1987), p. 132.

11. *Mark Twain's Autobiography*, 2 vols., (New York: Harper & Brothers, 1924), 2: 17.

12. See the introduction to Jim Zwick, ed., *Mark Twain's Weapons of Satire* (Syracuse: Syracuse University Press, 1992).

13. Ibid., p. 20.

CHAPTER THREE

1. Paine, *Mark Twain, A Biography* 2:724.

2. Budd, *Mark Twain, Social Philosopher.*

3. So Gregg Camfield persuasively contends in his afterword to *The Gilded Age* (New York: Oxford University Press, 1996).

4. He was named Eschol Seller in the first printing, but after a man named Eschol Seller turned up to protest the use of his name, he became Beriah, and then Mulberry Seller in subsequent appearances.

5. Paine, *Mark Twain, A Biography*, 1:540.

6. Ibid., 1:540–41.

7. "Introduction," *The Adventures of Tom Sawyer* (New York: Oxford University Press, 1996), p. xxxvi.

8. Quoted in the material prefatory to *The Prince and the Pauper* (Berkeley: University of California Press, 1979), p. 16.

9. De Voto, *Mark Twain's America*, p. 277.

10. Fiedler's and Turner's commentaries are appended to the 1980 Norton edition of the novel edited by Sidney E. Berger.

1. In his introduction to *Mark Twain, Christian Science* (New York: Oxford University Press, 1996), p. xxxvi.

2. Introduction to Mark Twain, *The Diaries of Adam and Eve* (New York: Oxford University Press, 1996), p. xxxvi.

3. Afterword to Mark Twain, *The $30,000 Bequest and Other Stories* (New York: Oxford University Press, 1996), p. 5.

4. *Twain-Howells Letters*, 1:11

5. This summary closely follows that of Paine, 2:852–54. The Petition, to be found in *The £100,000 Bank-Note and Other New Stories* (New York: Oxford University Press, 1996), was first published in 1897 and was so widely reprinted it reached the Queen herself. Some years later when Twain was introduced to Prince Edward, he took delight in the Prince's insistence that they had met before when Twain was atop an omnibus on Oxford Street wearing a gray coat with flap pockets.

6. De Voto, *Mark Twain's America*, pp. 314, 316.

7. Paine, *Mark Twain, A Biography*, 3:1157.

8. De Voto, *Mark Twain's America*, p. 358.

9. *Twain-Howells Letters*, 2:663.

10. Afterword to Twain's *Merry Tales* (New York: Oxford University Press, 1996). Robinson is citing James M. Cox's justly influential *Mark Twain: The Fate of Humor* (Princeton: Princeton University Press, 1966).

11. In *Mark Twain's Library* (Boston: G. K. Hall & Co., 1980) 2 vols., Alan Gribben finds that Twain owned Crane's *The Monster and Other Stories* (1899) but not *The Red Badge of Courage*.

12. Justin Kaplan, *Mr. Clemens and Mark Twain* (New York: Simon and Schuster, 1966), p. 358.

13. Paine, *Mark Twain, A Biography*, 3:1254.

14. Cox, *Mark Twain: The Fate of Humor*, p. 21n.

15. De Voto, *Mark Twain's America*, p. 265.

16. Paine, *Mark Twain, A Biography*, 2:747.

17. William Dean Howells, *My Mark Twain* (New York: Harper & Brothers, 1910), p. 169.

18. Ade is quoted by Beverly R. David and Roy Saperstein on p. 22 of their essay on illustrations appended to *Roughing It* (New York: Oxford University Press, 1996).

BIBLIOGRAPHICAL NOTE

Quotations from works by Mark Twain—either book-length or stories and sketches—are identified by title. All other quotations are identified in the endnotes.

The literature on Mark Twain is enormous. A useful overview is provided by Shelley Fisher Fishkin in the "Bibliographical Essay" included in the *Historical Guide to Mark Twain* (New York: Oxford University Press, 2002), which she edited.

INDEX